Polyphony Lit

The Best High School Writing from Around the Globe

Publisher: Polyphony Lit
Evanston, Illinois

Polyphony Lit 2018 Staff

Executive Director
Katie Scullion

Business Manager
Holly Kawula

Co-Founder/ Managing Editor
billy lombardo

Print Design
Tamara Fraser

Front Cover Image
Richelle Gribble

Board of Directors
Mary Bisbee-Beek
Francine Friedman
Beth Kohl
Dagmara Kokonas
John C. Lillig
Maggie Scheyer
Donna Seaman

Advisory Board
Stuart Dybek
Jennifer Egan
Betsy Franco
Edward Hirsch
Alex Kotlowitz
Chang-rae Lee
Jim McManus
Gary Shteyngart
Elizabeth Taylor
Scott Turow

Interns
Riley Grace Borden
Anya Chabria
Tyler Chodera
Emmy Chou
Izzy Chou
Isabella del Hierro
Dana Dykiel
Isabella del Hierro
Kelly Farley
Mari Kramer
Jodie Meng
Stephanie Racker
Jack Zucker

Editor Workshop Instructors
Jim Joyce
Ann McGlinn
Frank Tempone

Galleys Editors
Rose Branson
Isabelle del Hierro

Editor-in-Chief
Isabelle del Hierro

Co-Editor-in-Chief
Rose Branson

Executive Editors
Olivia Baker
Marleigh Belsley
Lily Campbell
Emily Cho
Isabella Cho
Brianna Chou
Briannah Cook
Cameron Cozz

Dana Dykiel
Maggie Eames
Kelly Farley
Sophia Feinerman
Joseph Felkers
Jessica Flohr
Amy Gersten
Cia Gladden
Anna Guzman
Hailey Hurd
Lara Katz
Robert Kelly
Pauline Paranikas
Stephanie Racker
Lauren Salzman
Grace Scullion
Lydia Sidrys
Georgia Souleles
Lucy Spahr

Genre Editors
Morgan Almasy
Kristen Altman
Alice Bolandhemat
Riley Borden
Kaela Brandt
Summer Crown
Josephine Daab
Kate Fawcett
MacKenzie Guynn
Emanne Khan
Julia Kinder
Morgan Kmety
Alec Kotler
Mari Kramer
Hyung Seo Lee
David Lee

Julia Maring
Jodie Meng
Grace Miller
Theodora Moldovan
Eva Nikitovic
Amanda Pyne
Julian Riccobon
I'deyah Ricketts
Noa Rosenberg
Josh Schlacter
Landon Smith
Rebecca Wanger
Katherine Williams
Karena Yan
Lily Zhou

Second Readers
Amanda Aprati
Isabella Aviles
Stuart Baker
Emma Beier
Paakhi Bhatnagar
Alyssa Brown
Eliza Bufferd
Nina Burik
Valerie Ceron
Iris Chen
Tyler Chodera
Addie Daab
Hannah Davis
Katherine Du
Abby Dutta
Julia Fairbank
Nadia Farjami
McKenna Fellows
Jocelyn Gao
Alex Gassel

Lydia Hahm
Katrina Herrera
Allison Henry
Mina Kim
Anthony Kolton
Maya Krainc
Serena Lin
John Liu
Yuqing Liu
Margaret Lu
Qinyi Ma
Vedika Mandapati
Rashann Nance
Amaya Oswald
Max Paik
Emily Perez
Cate Pitterle
Valentina Reetz
Tanay Rishi
Isabel Salvin
Tanya Singh
Anisha Sonti
Spencer Spahr
Reith Taggart
Patrick Tong
Michelle Tu
Rushil Vellala
Divya Venkatraman
Tamara Wallace
Lily Weaver
Lydia Wei
Sidney Wollmugh
Li-Anne Wright
Jaimie Yue
Jeffrey Zou

First Readers
Akrit Agarwal
Adil Alvi
Ore Amosu
Zoha Arif
Shridhar
Athinarayan
Karina
Belotserkovsky
Freya Buison
Michelle Cai
Adriana Carter
Victoria Choe
Evan Crosby
Jenny Doan
Ashley Duraiswamy
Sebastian Giordano
Casandra Gutierrez
Akshat Jain
Jenna John
Alex Jones
Dina Katgara
Dante Kirkman
Blisse Kong
Chelsea Kwak
Sarah Lao
Benjamin Le
Katie Lee
Michelle Li
Jeffrey Liao
Camille Lorie
Uma Menon
Alia Nathani
Noreen Ocampo
Jane Oh
Amika Sethia
Anya Shukla

Emmaline Teska
Naomi Tomlin
Nicole Tong
Paramita
Vadhahong
Elizabeth Wang
Jennifer Wang
Ellen Wu
Grace Yue
Cindy Xiong

3

Table of Contents

5

Isabella del Hierro

Editor-in-Chief

Capturing the Moments

Even as a high school student, it seems that as I grow up, time continues to advance at an exponential rate. This year, with the awareness that college is quickly approaching, it feels necessary to look back and reflect on the individual moments that have made up my life thus far. Some evoke sentiments of joy, others of sorrow, peace, or disgust – above all, though, they are short-lived.

I see writing as a way to memorialize these fleeting moments and the knowledge gained through the thoughts, emotions, and physical sensations that constitute them. Through writing, an experience that is temporary and personal can be transformed into something permanent that can be shared. *Polyphony Lit* is a grand collage of moments deemed worthy of being immortalized. Every piece is an opportunity to explore a new psyche through the creative structures that compose it, the little abnormalities that make it authentic. Through *Polyphony Lit* we, the readers, can experience for ourselves the triumphs, downfalls, keen observations and innermost reflections of young people around the globe, and learn from them.

For this reason, there is so much to gain by being a part of the *Polyphony* community. I feel incredibly fortunate to have been an editor for just over three years now, and with each new volume, I am amazed at the deep insights and unique perspectives put forth by my peers. However, *Polyphony* is not only sustained by the courageous authors who share their most personal moments with us in hopes that we might learn something; it also thrives due to our incredible editorial staff, whose thoughtful commentary continues to push forward the quality of our magazine, Katie Scullion, our executive director, Holly Kawula, our business manager, Billy Lombardo, our co-founder and managing editor and a very countable number of other adults who work behind the scenes, and our readers who are willing to open their minds and hearts. All of you are an integral part of this magazine, and I thank you sincerely for making this volume of *Polyphony Lit* a reality.

I am beyond proud of how far we have come in just the past few years, and I have no doubt that an even brighter future awaits. It is our dream to continue expanding our global community of voices, for this is the heart of *Polyphony* as well as its namesake. These young authors are thoughtful, capable, and worthy of attention. If you want proof, just turn the page.

7

Kelly Farley

Intern

The Beautiful Blue
Butterflies of Writing

Sometimes I read bits of writing that transform my feelings into words so perfectly that I wish I could've written them myself. That happens a lot with *Polyphony Li*t – not just with pieces but also with commentary and internal notes (I'm looking at you, person who compared a piece to scrambled eggs). And it happened with the quote above, which currently overlooks my cluttered desk. I find my eyes darting toward it when I procrastinate an especially complicated piece of writing by watching yet another video of a puppy eating peanut butter.

For me, the hardest part about writing is starting. I find myself typing and retyping an introduction, only to keep backspacing it because it's just not good enough. Reading great writing like that in this edition of *Polyphony Li* is mesmerizing, transformative, and downright enthralling. But it's also intimidating. I want my first drafts to be as good as everything I've read, so I end up not even starting them and scroll through Instagram instead. Especially when I first joined *Polyphony*,
I'd open Submissions Manager and skim over the sophisticated literary terms in the previous editor's comments and be unable to start my own for the fear of not writing anything good enough. I couldn't give myself the permission to write trash when everybody else around me was writing treasure – or at least looked like they were.

In this edition of *Polyphony Li*, you will see what I like to call the beautiful blue butterflies of writing. Look at the butterfly on our cover. It's captured in a moment of complete serenity. And it's all too easy to forget about what preceded this moment. We don't see the ugly caterpillar, squirming around on the ground. We don't see the butterfly first learning how to fly – and falling. We don't even see the butterfly flapping its wings as it still struggles to stay afloat. In short, what we aren't seeing is the process: the first draft scrawled on a napkin smeared with lipstick, the unnamed file that you're too scared to share with the world, the I-thought-it-was-perfect-but-it's-now-all-marked-up draft stained with tears. And this process isn't just limited to writers. Editors have the same issues, too, even if it can feel like you're the only caterpillar on the ground looking up at all beautiful butterflies and thinking you'll never join them.

That's why Riley Grace Borden and I started up the new *Polyphony* blog Voices. We want to put a spotlight on the caterpillars, instead of just the butterflies. An entire section of the blog is dedicated to #thestruggleisreal, where we discuss some of the hardest things about writing and editing, like writer jealousy and editing something you don't understand. Through editors and writers sharing their stories, we can see how we all feel like we're writing trash sometimes. We can feel okay with our trash. Most importantly, we can learn how to turn that trash into treasure.

As you look at all of the beautiful blue butterflies in the following pages, remind yourself of everything that came before. What's even more beautiful than butterflies are their metamorphoses.

billy lombardo

Co-Founder/Managing Editor

Another New Year

So many times in the year, I find myself looking at another temporal marker as an opportunity to reflect on the year behind and the year ahead. New Year's Day is probably biggest of these markers, of course, and birthdays are another. And I've been tied to the academic calendar for a half century now, so the academic year is yet another measure of the passage of time. There's a kind of loneliness (which is not to say unjoyful) that runs like thread through these markers – something about the occasions call for solitary reflection, reflect apart from others.

A fourth marker for me, though – and the one that distinguishes me from most of the rest of the world – comes every summer when it's time to lay out the new issue of an annually published magazine. For me, that magazine is the one you're holding in your hands, *Polyphony Lit*. And despite the fact that this distinguishes me from everyone else in the world, there is no loneliness to the reflection this annual even urges forth.

Every June and July for fourteen years now, most of the daytime hours I haven't spent on my own writing, I've spent preparing that year's volume of *Polyphony Lit* for publication. If I'm not reading the submissions our editors have been acting on since the previous July, I'm forwarding them to one of more than a hundred Crunch Time editors, contacting contributing writers and poets to inform them of their acceptance, inviting writers and poets from the grown-up world to judge submissions for our Claudia Ann Seaman Awards for Young Writers, or working with our in-house editors as they correspond with our poets and writers in fine-tuning their work for final publication.

Whether the submissions are publication-ready or in need of minor revisions, or they're the raw and underdeveloped first drafts of writers and poets in the first blush of their writing lives, every one of them is a song, a crying out of some occasion that desires and deserves voicing.

I know what it's like to sit at the table and wrestle to language the thing within, and I know what it's like to feel like you've done it. And though my writing, teaching, and coaching have all added greatly to the richness of my life, when all is said and done, I don't think anything I have done professionally is as important as this. Nearly every day, I am reminded of the impact our editors

. . . . ➤

have on their peers around the world.More than 13,000 times over the past fourteen years, some young poet, essayist, fiction writer, in one of more than sixty countries has opened an email from us that contains evidence that their cries, their songs, have not only been heard, but they've been read and re-read, they've been attended to, pored over, commented on.

It's more than just this attentive listening that feeds the soul of the young writer, though. There's something beyond thrilling that happens when the poet sits down again at the table, equipped not just with a greater sense of craft, but with the understanding that they have peers around the world who are intensely interested in helping them grow as writers, and they are not alone. They are a part of a global literary community. They are very much not alone.

11

billy lombardo

Announcing the Winners of the 2017 & 2018
Claudia Ann Seaman Awards for Young Writers

Polyphony Lit and the Community Foundations of the Hudson Valley are pleased to announce the winners of the Claudia Ann Seaman Awards for Young Writers.*

* Until this year, the Claudia Ann Seaman award winners were selected a year after their publication in Polyphony Lit. *This year, in order to shift to a more timely process, we are awarding both 2017 and, to be timely, the 2018 awards. To read the 2017 winners, see print Volume XIII published in 2017 or view online at www.polyphonylit.org. The winners for 2018 can be found in this issue.*

Claudia Ann Seaman Award winners are marked throughout *Polyphony Lit* with this symbol.

Our 2017 & 2018 CLAUDIA ANN SEAMAN AWARDS JUDGES

Kenyatta Rogers, *Poetry*

Kenyatta Rogers is a Cave Canem Fellow and has been twice awarded scholarships from the Breadloaf Writers' Conference. He has also been nominated twice for both Pushcart and Best of the Net prizes, his work has been previously published in or is forthcoming from *jubilat*, *Vinyl*, *Bat City Review*, *The Voltaand PANK*, among others. He is an associate editor of *RHINO Poetry* and currently serves on the creative writing faculty at the Chicago High School for the Arts.

Jeremy Wilson, *Fiction*

Jeremy T. Wilson is the author of the short story collection *Adult Teeth*. He is a former winner of the Chicago Tribune's Nelson Algren Award for short fiction, and his stories have appeared or are forthcoming in literary magazines such as *The Carolina Quarterly*, *The Florida Review*, *Hobart*, *Sonora Review*, *Third Coast* and other publications. He teaches creative writing at The Chicago High School for the Arts.

Mary Wisniewski, *Creative Nonfiction*

Mary Wisniewski is the author of *Algren: A Life*, the story of the brilliant but troubled Chicago novelist Nelson Algren. It won the 2017 Society of Midland Authors award for best biography and the Chicago Writers Association award for best traditional non-fiction. She is a columnist for the *Chicago Tribune*. Wisniewski also teaches non-fiction creative writing for the Newberry Library seminar program and the Northwestern University Summer Writers' Conference.

2017 Claudia Ann Seaman Awards for Young Writers

POETRY
Judge Kenyatta Rogers

Winner: **Chickadees**, by Grace Guiney,

Royal Bay Secondary, Victoria, British Columbia

The crouched cat, seemingly ready to attack, reflects back to the title and the poem takes a very interesting turn with bringing in melanoma. There are lots of things very static in this piece, but the threat of danger is still very present. The poem uses the grandpa and cat as figures in the poem, but are also used as an opportunity to meditate the ideas of both chaos and peace.

Runner-up: **Death is a Girl**, by Caitlin Hubert,

Chicago High School for the Arts, Chicago, IL

The allusions to both religion and mythology work beautifully, here. Death comes across as not contained to any particular person but also as feminine, wanted and desired, but also not. The bleeding title, "death is a girl/and she's tired," introduces the poem and gives readers an access to navigating these complexities.

Runner-up: **A Study in Consciousness**, by Nicole Tota,

Cherokee High School, Marlton, NJ

So many great and stunning images in this poem: "how to land a droplet of dew on a leaf," "if the smudge stays it always stays," and the idea of "an overused eyelid," all strike me as weird and marvelous. The associative movements between images to get at humanity are fresh and surprising.

13

FICTION
Judge Jeremy Wilson

Winner: Lake, by Caylee Weintraub, Mariner High School, Cape Coral, FL

In "Lake," siblings "imagine what it would be like to have webbed feet," and mothers can have scars that "look like gills," and fathers can "make rivers" where none exist. Water connects this family, but while the children wish to suspend time, to float perhaps forever, to transform into something aquatic, the lake is "drying up." The author uses the image of the lake deftly to illustrate the simultaneous push and pull of family, its ability to lift us up above the water and pull us down beneath the waves. The prose doesn't bubble or bloat, but cuts quickly to the most striking detail. "The moon stuck out like a knuckle." "Tilapia flee from our kicking feet." "His eyes dark and glossy like tapioca pearls." The story is like getting out of the water on one of those late summer days, where the chill on your goosebumped skin tells you fall is only minutes away.

First Runner-up: Good as New, by Martin Chan,
Wen Hua Senior High School, Taichung City, Taiwan

Second Runner-Up: Woman, by Heather Laurel Jensen,
Red Mountain High School, Mesa, AZ

CREATIVE NONFICTION
Judge Mary Wisniewski

Winner: Up, by Noa Rosenberg, Latin School of Chicago, Chicago, IL

This essay begins in a light and deceptively simple way – a young girl is up late, taking food from the fridge, enjoying being the only one awake in the house. But it leads into something more complex – the cultivation of memory, and the realization that the hardest parts of life are the ones that teach. It pledges a commitment to truth through writing.

Runner-Up: The Spaces Between, Emily Dehr

14

2018 Claudia Ann Seaman Awards for Young Writers

POETRY
Judge Kenyatta Rogers

Winner: **The Gender Dysphoria Sestina**, by Clio Hamilton, page 129

Lehman Alternative Community School, Ithaca, NY

Sestinas can be hard to pull off without sounding super redundant. How do you use a word, but make it new and do something different when it's repeated? This poem does is a lot, and creates the type off meditation and obsessions sestinas are known for. Add the topic and we get a poem which portrays an obsession in content, thought, and emotion.

Runner-up: **California Luck**, by Dana Chiueh, page 34

International Bilingual School, Hsinchu, Taiwan

The speaker's vision of an ideal life takes on what I'll call a contemporary California pastoral. The speaker ends up with a vision not much better than an existence and history they want to escape: death, alcoholism, and general human cruelty.

Runner-up: **Because of the Pear,** by Maia Siegel, page 62

Community High School, Roanoke, VA

A poem of defiance. The speaker consciously does things contrary to what you expect, here. The early images of putting an egg in a tomato play up on this quality of the speaker. The play with colors, food, and liquids are masterfully controlled.

FICTION
Judge Jeremy Wilson

Winner: **Drain**, by Clio Hamilton, page 131

Leman Alternative Community School, Itacha, NY

"Drain" works on you like a pill, slowly releasing its potency in expertly crafted details dropped at just the right moment. The cumulative effect mimics the main character's burgeoning awareness, "like the time she found Mom's breast." A startling and instantly intriguing image. The language is sharp and original: "the surface [of the lake] was pitted and translucent in places, like milk." "Maybe some shrimpy, scuttling thing found her skull and was living inside it." The story is devoted to exploring smallness in all its forms, the feeling of smallness, small things like tiny bald spots, and physical smallness. The main character feels small enough to be wrapped in a burrito, and by implication, small enough to be sucked down a drain. How does one navigate the world when your parents and everyone around you seem to take up so much space?

15

FICTION (cont)

Runner-up: *Advanced Fiction,* by Paul Michaud, page 197
Nashville, Tennessee

Runner-Up: *Turtleboy*, by Julian Riccobon, page 120
Pennsylvania Virtual Charter School, Pittsburgh, PA

CREATIVE NONFICTION
Judge Mary Wisniewski

Winner: *A Matter of Fact,* by Victoria Carl, page 138
Booker T. Washington Magnet School, Montgomery, AL

This essay speaks of the shame surrounding food and weight, and how thoroughly it permeates the writer's life and search for identity. The writing is clear, honest and sometimes devastating. The line about how a woman is "seen or heard or felt or tasted; we only exist in parts" shows a strong feminist awareness. It is a work of remarkable promise.

Runner-Up: *Ambiguous Truths,* Dana Dykiel, page 154
Acton-Boxborough Regional High School, Acton, MA

Runner-Up: *Blue Earth*, Max Hunt, page 37
Northpoint Christian School, Southaven, MS

16

About the 2019 Claudia Ann Seaman
Awards for Young Writers

The Claudia Ann Seaman Awards for Young Writers were created by the Seaman family in memory of their daughter and sister, a young poet. The CAS Awards acknowledge excellence in poetry, fiction, and creative nonfiction. The guidelines for the 2019 CAS awards are as follows:

Open to: All students in grades 9 - 12

Submission: Each participant may submit a total of three works: poems, stories, essays, or any combination (1500-word limit for fiction and creative nonfiction).

Deadline: Entries must be received by May 31, 2019

Cash Award: $200 award for each genre

Award Announcement: Fall

How to Submit: Submit your work directly to *Polyphony Lit* at www.polyphonylit.org.

All submissions entered via our online submission process at www.polyphonylit.org are automatically entered into the Claudia Ann Seaman Awards for Young Writers.

- Only submissions entered via our online submission process at www.polyphonylit.org will be considered for publication.
- Submissions must be original.
- Though we will consider previously published submissions for inclusion in Polyphony Lit, only submissions not published elsewhere will be considered for the CAS Awards.

Each entry must contain the following information:

- Student name, address, phone number, email address, year of HS graduation (Class of_____)
- School name, address, phone number
- Name and email address of student's English or writing teacher

17

About Our Name, Polyphony Lit
(p*uh*-**lif**-*uh*-nee **lit**)

In addition to the new cover art on this volume, you may have noticed we've gone through a slight name change: from *Polyphony HS* to *Polyphony Lit.* As we've grown, it has become increasingly important for the title of our magazine to more readily define who we are.

Invariably, in sharing the value of their work with others, our editors have had to explain that we are not an actual high school – though we are an organization devoted to high school writers and editors, all of us at *Polyphony Lit* feel we are also the most important literary magazine in the world, and the name change draws greater attention to our literary roots.

While we're on that topic, in our many discussions with editors and readers and board members about the possibility of a name change, one of the things we kept returning to was the importance of keeping the word *Polyphony* in our title. It comes from the Greek *polyphonos*: "having many sounds or voices."

About our Cover

Richelle Gribble creates mixed media paintings and drawings, prints, videos, puzzles and sculptures. Her artwork is inspired by concepts of virality, ecology, networks, group dynamics, and social trends that connect us all. She earned a BFA in Studio Arts from the Roski School of Art and Design with dual minors in Social Entrepreneurship and Marketing at the University of Southern California. Richelle is the winner of the 2016 Grand Prize Award for solo exhibition and representation at JONATHAN FERRARA GALLERY with inclusion in Art Market San Francisco, Texas Contemporary, and Miami Project. Her work has been exhibited on LED screens in Times Square; Christie's Salesroom Rockefeller Center; Fisher Museum of Fine Arts; John Wayne Airport; Planet Labs, and more. Works have been acquired by Tides Institute and Museum of Art, Kala Collection, USC's Art & Trojan Traditions Collection and has also flown (her art, that is) to space aboard Blue Origin's space system. Work presented in a TEDxTrousdale talk "What is our Role within a Networked Society?" and published in The Creator's Project, The Atlantic, and VICE Magazine.

Wo/ander

The title of the cover image of *Polyphony Lit* 2018 is Wo/ander. A collage of various images of organic material composed in a mystical landscape, it is inspired by the playful act of wondering and wandering in nature, celebrating the limitlessness of exploration.

You can learn more about Richelle and her work at www.richellegribble.com.

About Us

Polyphony Lit is an international student-run literary magazine for high-school writers and editors. We invite high school students worldwide to submit to us and/or join us as editors. The distinguishing feature of *Polyphony Lit* is that our student editors provide editorial feedback to every single submission we receive.

We offer three awards for excellence in writing through the Claudia Ann Seaman Awards for Young Writers, one each in poetry, fiction, and literary non-fiction and we publish an annual volume of the best writing we receive annually.

Workshops teaching the craft of literary editing are open to all high school students. An online course will be released in late 2018.

Polyphony Lit is a 501(c)3 non-profit organization (2008), incorporated in the State of Illinois.

Our Mission

Our mission is to create a high-quality literary magazine written, edited, and published by high school students. We strive to build respectful, mutually beneficial, writer-editor relationships that form a community devote

Our Beliefs

We believe that when young writers put precise and powerful language to their lives it helps them better understand their value as human beings. We believe the development of that creative voice depends upon close, careful, and compassionate attention. Helping young editors become proficient at providing thoughtful and informed attention to the work of their peers is essential to our mission. We believe this important exchange between young writers and editors provides each with a better understanding of craft, of the writing process, and of the value of putting words to their own lives while preparing them for participation in the broader literary community.

History

Founded in 2004, we are now more than 15,000 submissions from 62 countries and 50 states. We are homeschools and public schools and private schools. Co-founders Paige Holtzman (Latin School of Chicago '06) and Billy Lombardo are proud of what they started.

Originally called *Polyphony HS*, the first years were funded with support from the Latin School of Chicago. For several years now, we have been a federally recognized, 501c3 non-profit organization. We changed our name in 2018 to *Polyphony Lit*.

Our Future

Our mission and belief remain as relevant and important as ever. We never cease to be astounded by the number of teens online seeking to feed their hunger for literary engagement. In 2018 a new management team, Katie Scullion and Holly Kawula, began working behind the scenes with co-founder Billy Lombardo to build a more robust platform with deeper content to meet demand.

Our new blog, "Voices: 0% phony, 100% lit" was dreamed up and constructed by a team of high school students in the summer of 2018 and will provide another means for the thousands of teens who engage with us to be engaged and build community. Soon we will be launching our workshop, "How to be a Literary Editor" via an online platform for students worldwide. And our executive student editors are creating a new web series, "Real Writers Talk."

Maxwell Paik

Half Moon Bay High School, Half Moon Bay, CA

Summertime Poems

In the past three days, I have written 73 poems; that number jumps to 112 if you include the poems written by the night sky that I translated, but I don't count those because they were sloppy, had commas that made no sense, lines broken in all the wrong places.

By my count, 4 of those poems were about consumerism; or about the problems of consumerism, or about the unavoidableness of consumerism, each of those ended with some version of *irony is the anti-beauty*, which I believe is true in a dooming sort of way, a bit like a genetically inescapable disease, shared by the entire human race, a bit like self-centeredness or death.

Only 2 of the poems were love poems; that's less than 3% of my metaphorical output dedicated to love; make of that what you will.

Five poems were about baseball. My favorite baseball poem was titled *How Baseball was Invented,* and ended with a child smashing a cupcake with the snapped neck of her father's Gibson. The other 4 poems were about specific players. They were minimally homoerotic in nature.

Of the 11 poems dedicated to someone or something dead, only 2 were about deaths I didn't know personally. The poem titled *If David Foster Wallace Were Still Alive* was a bit too arrogant for my taste – which doesn't make sense because I felt very small and sad and not-arrogant when writing it. The only stanza whose skeleton would survive initial edits went like this:

> *If David Foster Wallace were still alive,*
> *would he have finally gotten around to writing his long-anticipated*
> *essay, complete with 22 footnotes and exactly two footnote-footnotes,*
> *on what it's like to be a man who made himself rich,*
> *worth five million dollars even a decade after he took his last breath,*
> *by selling anti-consumptionist writings?*

The other poems to the dead were very short; I didn't mean for that, but at some point, in a way all-too-relevant to the subject matter, they just ran out of steam.

I wrote a single, poorly-constructed haiku; I couldn't quite squeeze the full meaning of *hopeless irrationality* into seven syllables.

·········➤

25 poems were about math in some way; the best line was a play on words and went like this: *It's cosmic and beautiful and confusing, you can see-can't you.*

The rest of the math-based poems made me question my belief that the humanities and mathematics are not only reconcilable but codependent.

Three of the poems were about anxiety; they were the only ones that overdid it with imagery and metaphor. My anxiety was at points described as both like drowning and like floating, like being stuck and being fully and frighteningly free; like my biggest enemy and like something ingrained deep within me like height or shoe size. The only worthwhile thing I had to say centered on a metaphor about the sea, which involved something I learned long before I knew what a panic attack was: *If you're caught in a rip current, swim parallel to the shore.*

There were 6 poems which followed characters or narrative; each was about a young adult, lost and confused and dead tired of their life being handed to them in bubble-wrap.

I have since deleted 16 poems, and that number seems only to be growing.

. . . .

Don't be fooled by the playfulness of this one. So much going on beneath.

Max Paik is a senior at Half Moon Bay High School in Half Moon Bay, California. After graduating in 2019, Max hopes to attend a four-year college and live a life of travel and adventure. When he's not writing, Max works at the town library and plays with his cats.

Adriana Carter

Academic Magnet HS, North Charleston, SC

Foreign Home

In December, the dust crept into my lungs
    and I tried to catch the plane back to July –

barefoot Philippine summer and scraped skin searing
in salt water – the last time my mother dreamt

of her roots, of the country that was once, and
maybe still is, her home. It's beginning to bleed

shades of purple in my memory. And I know
her language runs through my veins, but

I am still choking on the words. Still learning
how to dance the way *Lola* did,

my feet tripping over themselves, stumbling over
bamboo, my bones collapsing into debris

beneath the sweltering sky. Today:
my mother cooking lumpia in the kitchen,

mangoes rotting in the pantry. *Do you remember
picking ripe fruit during dry season? Feasting*

with family members I've never met?
Mother— the once tangible lilt of your accent

is fading. I think, perhaps, the dust
is beginning to settle in your lungs too.

, ,

"Foreign Home" is intimate and subtle. We aren't told about the
speaker's relationship with her homeland or her new home or her mother –
we can see it in the way she talks about them. It's beautiful, nostalgic, and
speaks of home in the nuanced way people feel but struggle to express.
I knew from "I tried to catch the plane back to July" that this was a keeper.

27

Adriana Carter attends Academic Magnet HS in North
Charleston, South Carolina with the class of 2019.
Adriana's writing has been nationally recognized by the
Scholastic Art and Writing Awards.

Maria Hiers

H.B. Plant HS, Tampa, FL

House Cat

I found the cat years ago, when it was raining outside. His face was blank and he shook with deprivation. He stared at me from under a bench, his tail curled around his body. I'd never had a pet, but I did have a mouse problem, so I brought him home.

The cat hunted mice for hours, mostly for recreation. They scattered around the house while he stalked them, eyes ablaze. He found all his fun in the chase.

He was ill-tempered and boorish, and he made me scratch his stomach when I was supposed to be working. I'd be writing, have the whole thing typed out, with only the conclusion left for me to figure out. He'd come around and climb onto my lap, his belly a thick knot of matted fur. It stunk of arrogance, and when I tried to comb it with my fingers, they'd get stuck.

We spent the days together, I an isolate entity, he a nuisance. I tasked myself with capturing emotion and delivering it onto paper. Intrusive sounds weighed upon me, burning the bottoms of my eyes. Awful insults, born of detrimental lack, struck the inside of my skull. I wanted to encompass everything, envelop all of it in one heavy whole. The cat watched as I became someone whose words were more than the alphabet could produce. His tail would flick, stupid and mindless.

He didn't like anything I wrote. One day he came in and my paper said:

> "And everything feels like this ◯ and when it feels like this it is no fun at all. I look like this ◯ and I write like it, too. This ◯ can easily become all outside and no inside. And I'm saying it has been ◯ too long now."

The cat saw my paper and said that no one would understand my paper and that if we had any more milk he would like it, thanks.

He drank the milk and told me that I struggled because The Rules say there has to be an end, but that I have never known Ending; only the hurdle of Beginning and the limitlessness of In Between. I asked him what he meant but he didn't elaborate: he only ambled off for his nap.

Often, I was overcome with unease, bereft of a thing intangible and nameless. To record what I was experiencing as language seemed impossible, but the compulsion pervaded me – I could not ignore it. It emptied into anxious spasms, results of misconceptions and unrealities, while the cat watched with dry distance.

However selfish, though, he took interest in my difficulties. In between licks of his paws, he said to know Ending one must dissociate from Beginning, and in my situation this meant I was to take control of my circumstances and remove anything that taunted its influence over me. To reclaim ownership of myself was to experience liberation. Image, self-expression, ideology – all things the cat instructed me to retrieve, then deviate from. According to him, it was my responsibility to cast myself into total and threatening uncertainty, and then drag myself out in the pursuit of transcendence.

Days went by as he ate more and more mice. An act of violent devotion, he left their mutilated bodies at my study door. He committed himself to the killing while I was left to rid my own house of the debris.

I realized the act of writing delineates from the author's accumulated consumption. I concerned myself with locating beauty and understanding it beyond the aesthetic intent. I went places where I could absorb media, art, literature, and expressions previously unknown to me. What I witnessed inflamed my interior and brought harsh stinging to my eyes. Then I had a thought that maybe what I was trying to find could not be analyzed or deciphered, and I neglected intellect in favor of resounding visceral emotions.

I discovered a troubling duality, the two concepts of order and chaos. What each comprised made sense, but I could not discern which I belonged to. I revealed this to the cat and he told me to align with numbers for their clasp of definition and structure. All I had was volition and disorder; the two are cellmates. I sacrificed both to a systematic manipulation of my mind. Modules of militant self-discipline overran me, their invasive and debilitating corruption purging and erasing.

The commencing of reconstruction: measuring everything indiscriminately, self-indoctrination. I had almost nothing, just my physicality and the want of anything. Thinking that the supervision of the numbers I was made of paralleled with a calm and orderly world was a dangerous philosophy that I observed with dogmatic adherence. I shed my skin and that was easy. What eluded me was emerging from beyond it.

29

Choosing the proportion and evenness of order caused the omnipresent discomfort inside of me to subside. The chaos of things larger than me (time, weight, anxiety, body) had wracked me for years. By restricting them to nothing more than numbers, I stripped them of their power to infiltrate and destroy. Their categorization enabled me to touch what had formerly escaped my reach.

· · · · · · · · ▸

(Selfishness balances altruism and heavy balances light and aching balances fulfillment and everything is balanced until the only thing that can balance that is destruction.)

If disregarded, control can transmogrify into despotism. I slipped heedlessly into this with the same drunken ignorance of a zealot eager for resurrection. An insatiable greed for order possessed me; I was forced to divorce with limitation because of excessive alarming behaviors. If my numbers betrayed me, I experienced a relapse of the devastating and torrential anxiousness I had fought passionately to evade. Naiveté instilled me with the belief that I was in charge. But the numbers multiplied; I was scrutinized, then subverted.

The numbers said,

"This amount is too much. That is not the right weight. The clock is off by one minute. We see you are late. You are becoming unbalanced and sinful."

So I said,

"_____."

The cat saw possibility for insurrection. Any opportunity to hunt down and subdue weakness was welcomed by his capricious and apathetic soul. He came to me with a List of Worrisome and Cruel Misdeeds. He said he would listen to any objections with impartiality. However, if he found punishment justified, I would be expelled from my house along with everything orderly and sacred.

The List of Worrisome and Cruel Misdeeds

I.   Defendant has attempted the capture of things beyond her, for instance: time, weight, anxiety, and body. Although valiantly intentioned, she failed to recognize that none of these institutions belong to her. By not respecting their indubitable boundaries she has violated intangible and esteemed concepts.

II. Defendant does not realize she suffered a necessary coup; that was retribution for devouring. Her stupidity is concerning and proves she is unfit for authority.

III . Defendant maintains the fanatical delusion that she will write something that will provoke, illustrate, allure, and conclude. While her ideas are ceaseless and refulgent, she has avoided pen, letting herself waste amongst the pretentious pseudo-intellectuals of her time.

· · · · · · · · ·▶

I raged with indignation; what contemptuous scorn from the mouth I myself had brought in! My heart quit in one minute, a moment which effortlessly permeated my immaculate and faultless atmosphere. For the first time I saw the world as a pious devout, with unwarranted attacks against my faith slung at me from far and wide. But I was no believer, and paralysis crept in as understanding broke down the fortification of my vanity.

My feet were cold and solid on the floor as I glanced around. Dead mice littered my squalid and untended house. I perceived my study door – wide open, beckoning – and shuffled into the room. I laughed,

The ◯ pages of my journal fluttered as I slammed the study door behind me. I left my house as an exiled wound. The last I saw the cat, he was perched sullenly on my windowsill. He looked at me with disdain, wrinkled his nose, and wandered back into the house.

. . . .

I love everything about this piece – voice, plot, concept – but the linguistic construction is absolutely stunning; Hiers' vocabulary reflects the rise and fall of psychological intensity – the drop from intricate abstract vocabulary to cold, flat, simple word choice when the narrator returns to reality/sanity. It's extraordinary.

Maria Hiers graduated in 2018 from H.B. Plant High School in Tampa, Florida. She likes satirical novels, spending money on herself, and going out with friends. She dislikes telling people she's an English major only for them to then ask if she wants to be an English teacher.

Dana Chiueh

International Bilingual School, Hsinchu, Taiwan

overexposure

golden hour: everything picture-perfect,
like the afternoon before we escaped east
boston, remember? midas-kissed sun in our eyes
casting the deepest foreshadows. you wouldn't know
it's summer from the sun going down so fast on us,
but there we were. nighttime, knee-deep in august,
by the harbor. a place on the way to becoming gentrified
becoming abandoned in the process. there's a certain ugliness
to abstraction, to night and light: the subway station
where two were shot dead back in january, the kind of place
that makes the channel 12 news. give me construction tarps
and i'll show you the messiness of reconstruction, but these boys
exist everywhere, boys who call themselves Kanye West, Josiah
from the south side, black jeans and flash cameras;

after hours, everywhere becomes a man's Americana.
the seedy underbellies of suburbia call us names we start
      to call ourselves –
mere exposure: the more times you hear something, the more
you believe it. it always sounded like they were catcalling
      someone else,
but the streets claim us for their own. regurgitate the
sweethearts, the baby girls, still sleeping in the back
of my throat, on the tip of my tongue,
cough up suds tasting more brainwash than reclamation.
i remember: "say cheese" to your canine teeth yelling "look at me"
and i think run, i think evolutionary widening of eyes to match a doe's
and boys who subsist on that surprise, all of us, out here
      on some breezy

32

sort of summer night (stock-photo happy tinted tabloid-sour with
the way hood boys read a gaggle of shorts like open invitations)
entrapment in tie-dye, on a concrete sidewalk. just keep walking.
make it to the next streetlight, let the yellow erode any leverage left
amidst the crabgrass, their brassy laughter spoiling the darkroom

where do you keep the flash photos of the girls who
say the wrong things, ruin everything? the rest of us keep our heads
down, like accepting an overexposed compliment, training our attention
on the slap of black flip-flops on bland pavement under moonlight,
the crunch of undissolved sugar between pressed teeth.
i drown my fear in the space between ice cubes clinking against
styrofoam.
every door too closed and the streetlights never on our side
the echo of taunts, of harsh light, sole witnesses.

this – the first iteration. the first women we've ever become.
ice melting by the time we stumble into dizzying fluorescence
but there are light leaks on my memory, as the T rushes past
tunnel vision: my voice cracks every time it remembers how
it failed me that night.

and now
deep night refrigerator lights and the moon
the same one that refused to illuminate our darkness

33

It's important. It's relevant. It's timely. And it's beautiful. It's rare to have this maturity
that maintains a teenage voice. Sophisticated yet intimate, soft-spoken yet hard-hitting,
beautiful but tragic – all balanced in a meditation on the American Dream.

Dana Chiueh

2018 Claudia Ann Seaman Award Runner Up for Poetry

california luck

When news broke of the broken
woman's carcass left behind a forest green
dumpster, I do not cry. I think of
my father's Stanford, scholarship-sent year
of laboratories and Church's Chicken and zero alcohol tolerance
something I'm blessed or cursed to inherit
even though it won't stop them asking Were you drinking?
Not even a little? It's June 4, the day between freshman
graduation trip and prom and I am sitting in class
listening to the world take each fragile sober breath;
her sorrys multiply in my chest cavity, falling to the floor
in a mess of crumbs. I think California is only for the lucky, the pavement
padded with the crunch of luckless bones. My father
speaks of the Trees reverently; solid California glow, fat
bean sprouts and cilantro-heavy broth in Mountain View –
cheap reminders of home.
But with each new incident another college brochure
is thrown in the trash. California
treated Brock Turner well, too.
What's left? we ask, as the American spirit lays naked,
unconscious, as the world goes by.

....

*The concept of the naked American spirit is a great presence in this poem –
personal and introspective on one end, and as big as America on the other.
Technical elements, such as enjambment, create an aesthetic that both jars and
moves the reader. The almost pastoral image that the reader is left with at the
end encourages contemplation, especially regarding how much protection one's
everyday cultural landscape offers when all the background noise fades away.*

jack o'lantern

love does not want this body,
does not want twisting, unfeeling,
spread out greedy just to make room for more surface area body,
some untouchable place
i am fully inhospitable and my palms are outstretched,
    wide open spreadeagle
begging in twilight,
shiny knuckles and blood-vessel eyes and voices soft like melons.
all i dream of is my heart leaving me and saying hallelujah
hallelujah to my body – every bruise a suicide note
each colorful crumple of exoskeleton a monument to my crushability.

to be a birch, a spirit floating free of peeling paper skin.
Mother, we asked only for perfection and now someone has
    had to do it for you
screaming your name they decorated me raw.
and struggle – no longer the most beautiful thing of perseverance,
heaves in time with the scoops in your microscopic universe,
take off your faith, your sweat-stained beliefs –
strip you of your god, who warned your mother about her unborn daughters
your god, who let this happen

you can't teach a pumpkin how to heal its carvings,
but it's like a cartoon, you see – a caricature
everything i will have lost by this time tomorrow, or in twenty years.

i am a ghost town tonight full of apologies for every resident who
almost made it out alive
they say Mother as I name them all,
and the piercing tongues leave me with nothing but windblown
eulogies lost in translation

. . . .

*"i am a ghost town tonight full of apologies for every resident who almost
made it out alive." There are pieces of this poem that shine like obsidian.*

Dana Chiueh

fallibility of memories

After Laura Kasischke

smooth as a memory:
the slippery lies we ran our tongues over
and over and over in our mouths
like rock candy, polishing worn
enough to believe in
even history was too careless to remember
our own, old gravity
dizzy with distortion;
real memories come out sandpaper.
enough to wear and be worn down
born too rough, but we stitch up the sides,
hating the fray

in my head, my dreams come fully formed
like imposter memories with iron grips.
water, on the other hand,
turns all stones smooth with time.
& every memory inevitably causes a beautiful
hurt, jagged piercing edges
worth the remembering.

....

This poem (especially the first stanza) grabbed me with its unique but accessible imagery. A tongue smoothing rock candy as a metaphor for convincing ourselves to believe in false memories: it's simple, raw, and new.

36

Dana Chiueh is a poet and writer attending the International Bilingual School at Hsinchu-science-park in Hsinchu, Taiwan. She grew up in East Setauket, NY. As a member of the Class of 2019, she is busy making the most of her high school years by watching paint-mixing videos or tweeting @danachewy.

Max Hunt

Northpoint Christian School, Southaven, MS

 2018 Claudia Ann Seaman Award Runner Up for Creative Nonfiction

Blue Earth

blue birth.

air conditioning: it snaps against the skin to dry the amniotic fluid, crust the newborn's face. already, in the womb, the baby understood: the dark, the light. so even now: the loss of safe, the newness of the pain. the face is scrunched, and palms and fingers, heels, and toes are blue; and baby's father tells the doctor, laughing, *it's so ugly, put it back*, but doctor doesn't laugh. the mother sucking ice and baby sucking breath; the baby fights for bits of its elusive oxygen for days beyond the birth. *but this is normal,* doctor says.

blue blight.

baby turns from blue to yellow. father gifts the jaundiced baby to the sun. impatient for the sky to rinse away the sick, the baby cries. the yellow skin around the eyes is crinkled with the loss of *safe.* so father shushes. baby *wai-ai-ails.* so father laughs and says to mother: *baby doesn't like the sky. afraid to fall into the blue and never come back down.*

blue earth.

crayons for the child: to color blue, the sky; to color water gray. correction from the father (pointing finger, tapping paper): *water should be blue, since it reflects the color of the sky.* although the child never saw the blue in water – ponds outside are muddied, gray – the child chafes the crayon on the paper. blue is blue and gray is blue and yellow, blue. So what else blue? so everything, the child concludes. and people, too; that is the loss. with *safe* a blurry smear amidst amalgamated colors, child asks: can people fall into themselves and never surface?

37

⋯⋯⋯➤

blue body.

the sound of blue encasing bones: a yipping puppy running to a street. so child chases yipping puppy. yipping puppy stops in street and *yip-yip-yips* at sky. event: a car. so child freezes: circumnavigates the skull, discovers how the cranium confines, the neurons' everlasting existential crises at their only job: to register the fear and pain, and finds in every corner of the skull – the blue – the blue – the blue – event: a car is screeching. car is swerving. child chases puppy from the road while yelling, tripping, falling – landing on both hands to slick the grass between the asphalt and a ditch – rolling over to be greeted by the blank face of the sky. and such a sacrifice: to offer up a child to the realization that the blue neglects to mourn the deaths of children that it births. the car meanders on, and dog will yip until it learns the art of giving up.

blue dream.

an event: the blue-born child closes eyes and dreams of drowning in a sky of blue. so child forgets to sleep. so child forgets to eat. so child forgets to not feel pain. so child forgets to be a child. but child remembers this: the blue, the loss of *safe*. so child tells the doctor: all my thoughts are ugly, put them back, but doctor doesn't laugh. *this isn't normal,* doctor says.

blue death.

but this is normal: sensations of dissociation in the child's bones; *but this is normal*: child looking for the thing that holds the body to itself, already knowing blue has pocketed the body's alveoli, shrouded them for death; *but this is normal*: child asking when each joint will finally reject its corresponding bones; *but this is normal*: tiny puppy made for yipping at the sky; *but this is normal*: sting of air against an open wound, and skin keeps searching for the oxygen the child lost at birth; *but this is normal*: child mouthing senseless mantras in an effort to forget about the airless color creeping back into the palms and fingers, heels and toes; *but this is normal*: to forget the child used to breathe before the body felt the blue between its bones.

blue blood.

so child asks: who was the first to color water blue? so crayons for the child, to color water gray – or green – or red – or gold – or clear – yes. why not clear – ? it snaps against the skin: the death of *safe* and death of *normal*; then, the birth of possibility. the child's need to rail against the sky. the body's revolution: thrusting red through arteries and giving life to child's lungs.

blue breath.

so even now: the dark, the light.

I have a soft spot for complex-wisdom rants like these. The chromatic theme seeps through every word, painting it all with sparing brushstrokes: a careless father, a child drowning in their own mind. The parallels between beginning and end are brilliant, begging, demanding what normal means.

39

Max Hunt is a member of the 2018 class of Northpoint Christian School in Southaven, Mississippi. He is currently a freshman at the University of Mississippi, where he may or may not double major in History and English. He doesn't know. Maybe he'll become a bubble artist, because those are cool.

Madeline Figas

Pittsburgh Creative and Performing Arts, Pittsburgh, PA

Dear Kyra, We're Only Beginning

Dear Kyra,
we're only beginning
to stutter step across alleys
and hold breaths
that aren't our own.
We still have a library of firsts,
midnight trains waiting,
conversations stuck on pause,
and mouthfuls of *I love you,*
but...

Kyra I once wrote you
a poem
about an ocean with no shore,
about the universe stretching,
how we were nothing
but dust.
You told me that we have only
tasted
a second of the world –
that this
is just the start.

....

No words wasted here in this simple, unpretentious, and imperfect love poem.
It's a whisper, wide-eyed, dark, and wise, that beckons you to listen closely.

40

Madeline Figas attends CAPA, a creative and performing
arts school located in Pittsburgh Pennsylvania. She's
in the graduating class of 2020. When she's not writing,
Maddie is either reading or playing soccer.

Anna Chen

Interlake High School, Bellevue, WA

pink is a shade of red

Is heat needed
to make rubies?

I've never known
the recipe, but
real cooks
don't need them,
right?

Don't think
about cooks.

I wonder how
to cremate a butterfly –

to spare or not to spare
the wings?

– and one day they said
my skirt was a mixture
of fuchsia and rose and
maybe mulberry, too?

No, it was blood-red –
they see pink in everything
winged.

I wonder what
they'd label the shiny skin
on my forearms:
blush or rose or
cotton candy?

Charred crimson, a
raw red rare. Pain when
you seared the stones
into your skin, pain when
they sandpapered them pink.

Will they taste sweetness or
will they pucker their lips
in disgust, in exasperation, in
some exotic flavor
of pity?

This one is really special. There are complexities within the text that bloom only with repeated reading; you have to give it time to seep in. I love the metaphor of rubies – with their fiery elegance – and the tone of the piece to express the speaker's struggle with femininity.

41

Anna Chen, a sophomore at Interlake High School in Bellevue, Washington, has been acknowledged both internationally and nationally by the Claremont Review and National Scholastic Art and Writing Awards. She founded and currently runs her school's creative writing club, and was named a Global Literacy Champion for starting a library in Malawi, Africa.

Coco Huang

Hornsby Girls' HS, Sydney, Australia

Grave of the Butterflies *

The lone tree stands in the town square,
gnarled branches like twisted hands
reaching; nestled in its joints,
a thousand maple-red leaves
sleep with folded wings.

A breeze chills the old moaning tree
that rubs its palms together for warmth;
Awake, crisp-veined leaves a-flutter
with lusty hues of rich red gold
enchant the wandering eye
and drown in its
abysmal black.

Now and again, a butterfly breaks free,
soars in sunlight and splendour
ascends with vigour
yet feels and knows
the dying of the
breeze.

There lies the valiant soul,
There lie all the brave;
The children, pink with wild delight
leave footsteps on their grave.

But not all children are lovingly scarved –
how he wishes that he were!
If only a trace of his mother's light touch,
swathed between the wool and fur –

He doesn't.

By the damp pit he kneels and prays
and stirs the ghost-leaves in their graves
with questions that no child should ask:
whether it hurts when butterflies die,
and where, and how,
and when, and why.

---

*It's Coco's gorgeous and heartful language here that creates the effective
duality of the piece – the juxtaposition of childlike innocence and loss.
It's delicate and substantial at the same time.*

Coco Huang is an Australian writer who graduated from
Hornsby Girls' High School in Sydney, NSW in 2017*. A
scientist at heart, she dabbles in music composition, art and
linguistics, and likes collecting bread clips. Her works have
cropped up in strange corners of the internet and in print.

43

* *Grave of the Butterflies was submitted before Coco's 2017 graduation.*

Blisse Kong

Ridge HS, Basking Ridge, NJ

Before it Melts

I am five
and I see the truck, with chips of pink on its surface.
"Mommy, let's go buy ice cream!"
Green bills in hand, the founder's face smiling back at me
I toddle with my best buddies to buy a super shiny cone
of fire truck red, vanilla white, and sky blue.
The sugar sticks to my hands
as I taste its unworldly sweetness.

Now I'm seven
with cartons of Ben & Jerry's stashed in my freezer.
The song of the truck, clopping playfully like horses' hooves
            on a summer day
wafts in as I do multiplication problems.
"Mommy, can I go buy a cone?"
"No, honey… We have ice cream at home."

I am eleven
Double digits, double the responsibility
I toss boxes of ice cream bars into the cart
and when we drive home,
The song, a little scratchier, a little more worn,
resonates through the neighborhood.
My sister, only five, asks,
"Mommy, I want ice cream!"
My mom sighs and murmurs,
"Next time."

I am thirteen
and I've said goodbye to my hometown
to leave for a new home
Bursting with those sparkling New England trees
Lush green lawns, stately brick houses
and all the neighbors' children
have gone off
to the Ivy Leagues.
I sit reading *Atlas Shrugged*
when the ghost of sound returns, tugging with it
a wistful story of carnivals
long past, popcorn long gone stale
by the melting of time from days
to months to years.
Cicadas chirp, the sweat clings to my back.
I laugh and ask, "Why would he come here?
No one here is going to buy ice cream
from him."

My youngest sister, only three,
begs mom for a cone
her eyes orbs of fragile innocence.
She runs out
and the ice cream man,
who never seems to age or change
no matter where I go,
Tells my mother why he comes
in the midst of those deliberate New England trees.

I am finally fifteen
old enough to drive
and get my own ice cream.
I sit studying for the SATs
and the windows are closed, the shades pulled down
as a blanket from the blazing wanderlust.
It's exactly 3:30.

45

· · · · · · · · ·▶

I brace myself for the chime
of the bell that only serves to remind me
of the fuchsia summer orchids
clamped under the darkness of pressure.

It drives to the end of the street, the song
screaming against its muffle and then
stops. The man drives around the bend
and back up the street,
completely silent save for
the rumble and creak of an experienced truck.

I close my eyes
at the thought of
the man, who came from a country melted into
oblivion by war, to one sprinkled
with the obscenely poor and the obscenely rich
all hiding behind roads caked with gold
in the hopes that his children
would one day be the buyers,
not the sellers

....

*I can sense the author peeling away layers with every stanza, slowly revealing
a deep and painful truth. And then the end comes and silently drops the mic
with a little twinkle of a smile and all I could think was "damn."*

46

Blisse Kong is a junior at Ridge High School in Basking Ridge,
New Jersey. As a member of the class of 2020, she hopes
she'll be able to develop a 20/20 literary vision through her
pieces. Blisse enjoys playing the violin and baking.

Nikki Velletri

Mount Saint Charles Academy, Woonsocket, RI

Immortalized in Contrapposto

There are very few parts of the summer
that concern us and I wish the wasting away
wasn't one of them. The way I heaved in
        shallow breaths outside the Louvre, the smell
of sweaty tourists clinging to my nostrils,
staples tickling my stomach with each
                inhale. They say you'd need a hundred
days to see it all. If I had that kind of time,
I'd be a little less *Winged Victory* – ancient,
faceless – and a little farther away
from France.

And maybe everything would look a little less
like dissolution: the glass and its spider-
        webbed skin cells, the pyramid's ghostly
hands – divine spires reaching upward
to stave off divine ends. People don't go
                to Paris unless they're in love or
dying, so we were asking for it to
end this way – begging really, folded dresses
leaving impressions on our thighs but mine
cutting straight through to bone.

If there was ever a version of this life where I live
long enough to become a doctor, I'd be the quack kind
        who whispers in comatose ears, tries to sew
fight into the cloth of a body.
        Acquiring anything requires a certain degree

· · · · · · · · ·▶

47

of desire. Surviving anything requires
        a whole damn ocean of it and hands
that don't burn when set aflame.

I walked the same hallway four times before
      my mother found me, clutching someone
else's topcoat and dreaming of my bed back
home. This is not the way the world should end,
chasing monuments under numbered sunsets,
        but there are only so many options
to choose from. The worst – my mother's hands
inside a body cavity, my shiny face
      and gaping mouth, opening again and again
like a gutted fish to spill empty recitations:
are you consumed with the way I almost
made it?

No, later that night on the Seine – the sugar-coated
fingers and the pulsing river, the dying bird on
the surface still flapping its wings. It wasn't over but
        it would be, a truth worse than the bleeding
out. The end had always existed, waiting
      between the paintings for me to slip into it.
Mona Lisa and I shared a wicked smile
before I left even though we're
not the same – she figured out
how to live forever.

. . . .

"Immortalized in Contrapposto" does exactly what the title says. It leaves you
stuck, in the middle, in the most beautiful of ways, straddling the lines
between prose and poetry, between comedy and tragedy, between the past
and the future; this one holds me in the best kind of suspension.

48

Somewhere in Louisiana

Summer in the bayou and everything's
Freudian. We dangle bare limbs over the edge
of the cruiser because nothing can hurt us
unless we will it to. Life doesn't exist
until we command it to the surface,
which is how we can sleep soundly with
our backs frying brown. The sun winks
as it slips from the skyline. Our bodies
belong to anyone who
needs them.

Three days in, I run out of socks. Clean water
doesn't exist here – the whole concept
of it. There's something charming in the way
everything runs back into something else,
alligators drinking the blood of birds they killed
a week ago, spit up from ceaseless sludge
to rot on the shoreline. Nothing can really escape
from the grips of the swamp, that heavy mirage
of heat and death. I almost stuck my feet in,
but my parents promised to wait
at the airport. And I think there must be
hundreds of bones lining the bottom
and I don't particularly want mine to rest
among them.

On the last day we burn our ruined shoes
because there's nothing worth saving,
anyway. We were definitely here for a reason
but I forgot to pack sunblock so that's all
I'll remember. All that I've forgotten is equally
important – the way I would have swam
through the muck for a single glass
of lemonade, how you vowed to rip

·········▶

Nikki Velletri

the sun from the sky. I wanted to leave
something behind – a mark in
the mud, a tiny skeleton –
but the wake behind the cruiser always
settles back into stillness. No one can really
live forever. I just didn't want to say it
out loud. Every unimaginable life
does not exist in some parallel
universe, but in this one.

. . . .

*The colloquial narration shortens the distance between audience and speaker. This
piece deserves to be published. Existentialism is tricky to execute well, but this author
does it seamlessly by creating a sense of indifference that is far from indifferent.*

Landscape Aflame

It is autumn now, and I forget to dream in
color. My dog vomits on the new carpet, says

it's time to think in the long term, but it is
my father's voice that comes out of her mouth

– how I would imagine his voice sounding,
anyways. It's funny how we do that,

we take the pieces of the nightmare and unlace
them until they fall just where we want them to.

Pick up the pieces, throw them down the staircase
until they fall just where we want them to. It is

September but I know winter is waiting for
me to leave the house, just like my mother, just like

the part of my brain still beating its fist
against the inside of my skull.

In the waiting, I grow tired of swallowing pills and
fucking, so now I do neither. Abstain. Cure-all.

I relish in it, my own body, tell my dog I couldn't
have said it better, and delete my entire contact book.

When I die, I would like to float out to sea,
if there's a body left to be found

········▶

Nikki Velletri

or made of me. And if there is a child – there may
be a child – leave her only the good dreams,

the dreams in full pigment.

. . . .

*"Landscape Aflame" has the hazy aura of a dream. The author clearly
understands how to weave together different ideas, voices, and tones, and,
with all of this, the work is one that practically demands a second read.*

Guest In-House Editor, Mikaela Ritchie

Nikki Velletri

From the Slums

Stirring at the border. Turns out I was still waiting
after all. For what I could not tell you. It's been
long enough that this loss doesn't resound with
anything present and yet I still return to it, to that
white stretch in my mind, to that ghostly morning
on the freeway with the sky stretched out in a sheet
of parchment, your face and the sky hollowed and
bruised, everything that followed.

The problem with memory is that it falters. And still
at this hour each car rumbling above the overpass
becomes a promise beckoning me to follow,
beckoning me into a life I can never shrug into and
I cannot run. Not anymore. So now I love nothing
but the easily disposed, remember nothing but the
easily forgettable, and that morning – once gilded,
once placed in my mind on some unreachable
pedestal – it's gone. Whiteout. So I will tell you

about the night. Because it was dark. Because I loved
you. Because I could never hope to forget the planes
of your face. And is that not what love is after all,
after every forked road has enslaved us – a last path
we wished never to arrive at?

It was past midnight. You had clambered behind
the counter in your uncle's little restaurant, made us
the strongest martinis I've ever had, told me how
our children would walk these same streets one day
and never believe we had escaped their frightful
invitations. And it was past midnight when
you pushed me in that rickety little shopping cart
all through the fishing district, all the old ladies
poking their heads out their windows to hail us
in a language I left behind years ago. And it was
past midnight when we slipped our fingers beneath

53

Nikki Velletri

the pulse of the nightlights, let them pulse inside
our bodies which we, of course, had already left
behind. Memory with it, memory nothing but
a salve now, the barest soothing to an ache of
its own creation. Can I say it now? Now that
no one is listening? I thought you'd make it.
I thought you'd make it, oh God, I thought
you'd make it –

The truth about memory is that I never wanted it.
Even then, beneath the purple lights, all the shops
shuttered in metal sheets and clothed in darkness,
your lips the reddest thing for miles, I wanted nothing
but a single, unequivocal moment of it. To later
point at it down the years, say that was happiness.

But nothing ends so neatly. All the things that slipped
into recollection: your bleeding knuckles on my
cheek; dancing on the roof's edge; the girls who
stopped when we passed, arrested by our joy;
waking in the middle of the night to find you
half-naked in the streets, watching the moon.

I never told you that I saw you. I saw you. Left you
standing in the road, open-palmed. In my mind
you're still there. And for what it's worth now –
after the train platform fell hallowed as a cemetery,
after your cheeks grew gaunt in the aftermath,
after dozens of baggies disappeared off bathroom
sinks and barroom countertops, after the inevitable
news inevitably reached me and I mourned
the city that would keep you far longer than
I would – I remember. I never looked away.

. . . .

*There is something enchanting about the imagery, about the block-paragraph
verse slicing into run-on sentences the way time cuts up memory. There's certain
beauty here, the gritty sort that serves as a testament to the human experience:
"I wanted...to later point at it down the years, say that was happiness."*

As I Might Miss

Your own desires besought you. Finding skin to be
the second most disposable object in any

given bedroom. No one wanted your charm or wholehearted
hunger, your voice that lulled the restless to sleep

and his body to your own as the answer to some
ineluctable promise; they wanted details.

You, a good soldier, incising every demanded piece.
Forgetting what you once imagined this life to be.

Somehow your body still astonished you, your heart still
affronted your mouth in its contradictions

and we loved your slanted gaze and lips, always quirking,
we wanted to know more. We wanted to press it

against our noses until we understood, until it
fell apart. Until it sunk into our skin

and we could call the story our own and how, in telling it
for years, we dragged your bodies for miles

caught beneath the back tires, us in the front seat singing
your love song and never minding

the strange thump that begged for a runaway ramp.
The night is falling in on itself, so

tell it again to remember. This time give me the slightest
variations so I can go to sleep and dream a better ending

· · · · · · · · · ➤

– I want two boys in love and no one has to pay for it,
I want two boys in love and I never have to feel like

it's the closest I'll ever get to the midnight phone call asking
for another chance or my mother's voice telling me

the world is a nightmare and love does not conquer
and to *come home baby*, to *come home soon*.

....

"As I Might Miss" is hauntingly beautiful. By invoking imagery of "us in the front seat singing / your love song," the poet reveals the desperation of the speaker, who longs for a story in which there are "two boys in love and no one has to pay for it." Love mostly doesn't have a happy ending, and this piece exposes the blissful ignorance of those who wish it did.

Nikki Velletri is a student in the Class of 2019 at Mount Saint Charles Academy in Woonsocket, RI. Her work has been recognized by the Alliance for Young Artists and Writers, the National Park Service, and *The Adroit Journal* and can be found in *Kingdoms in the Wild* and *L'Ephemere Review*, among others.

Alrisha Shea

State College Area High School, State College, PA

scatterbone knucklebone

scars trace railroad tracks over kalimba ribs,
    push them in and feel them spring back

    my side springs to attention but
        my back refuses form

        my teacher tells me vibrato will
            slide into place

            miraculously, impossibility
                slipping to possibility

(despite all evidence, i don't believe that)

    because each of my bones was retrofitted
    to my body;
    i am a hastily assembled model skeleton,
        a biology class demonstration of incompetence my
    maker flooded graveyards and
        threw my frame together;
        no regards to gender or jigsaw,
        my anatomy was creaky-jointed and out of tune from day one

    i am scared my writing is like my vibrato
        because as easily as a shoulder relocates
            it dislocates easier next time

57

so my knuckles writhe in time
        for now, but who knows how long my luck will hold?
            (attributing success to person
                is too scary to think about –
                    blame broken legs instead)

i've never seen my bones nor snapped them
        but i know they are already fractured all o'er
            and sucked dry of essence;
                like bothersome children
                    sipping dry drinks drier

lord, let my marrow last me another day;
                        i need to be good at something, just this once

. . . .

*There's a distracted urgency to the disjointed, scattered rhythm. The lines rattles
like bones, and the lack of punctuation on the last line lets its pleading desperation
linger with me longer. It crafts a web of broken artifice, only to open up into this
bare, human need. So beautiful and ugly, so at heart with my generation.*

Alrisha Shea is a member of the 2019 Graduating Class at
State College Area High School in State College, PA. They
are planning to go into Bioinformatics in undergraduate studies.
Their work is forthcoming in "Occulum" and other publications.
They can be found @alrisha_s on Twitter.

Vivian Parkin DeRosa

Communications H.S., Wall, New Jersey

Ragged

lean in and you'll smell
the corkboard on her breath
and see the pushpins on her skin
a desperate pining of her aspirations.
her dreams walk tightrope on her eyelashes.
but they told her that taxis don't smell
of hope and traced constellations
just dried playdough and maps with teriyaki
sauce stains right over the place
you need to go.
they told her that travel was not a galloping horse
hooves will never beat to the desire in her chest.
It's just another merry-go-round
certain to end where you started
and start where you end.
Everything she ever needed
is begging on the trim of her fingernails
but she cuts the edges off ragged
and pretends she is reaching for something else

I have a few questions, about this one, but I'm not sure I want them answered. All of the
senses are here, and two more – journey and pain – make strong bids to be added.

59

Vivian Parkin DeRosa is a writer, poet, and student at
Communications High School in Wall, New Jersey. She will
graduate in 2019. Her work has been recognized at the national
level by the Scholastic Arts and Writing Awards and has previously
appeared in the Huffington Post and other literary magazines.

Destiny Perkins

Pittsburgh Creative and Performing Arts School, Pittsburgh, PA

I Leave You with This Trauma

*'When two people have been close, you can say in Spanish that they were fingernails and dirt. **Eran una y mugre.** That's how close they were.'*

– A Cup of Water Under My Bed, Daisy Hernandez

My mother met Norman 'Stormy' Johnson while working at one of many nightclubs he owned on the east side of Pittsburgh and they began courting when I was four. I remember him vaguely as a broad, homely man draped in oversized black tee shirts and baggy dark blue denim, a chunky gold chain gleaming around his short neck. By September 21, 2005, my birthday and his, he'd disappeared. In his place, he left my mother, a swollen melon with long extending tendrils, bidding him good luck.

On July 17, 2006, Faith was born.

We never even hear his voice. One of the last words Faith learns to say is 'Da-da.' But even still, my mother won't call him out of his name.

My father has settled down. He welcomes his second child with his new wife four months after Faith is born and he's making plans of moving to Virginia. In phone calls, my mother demands to know what will become of my weekend visits to his apartment in East Liberty. She curses my father on lonely weekends when I'm sitting on the couch, waiting for him with a packed bag at my feet.

My mother whispers rumors of the throne Norman has built in the grimy streets of the East. There are ghosts of him in the backgrounds of Youtube rap videos, where he's shrouded by fine women and motorcycles. He stands stoic as his friends spit verses soaked in black blood. I find traces of him in the throng of his other children, who my sister has only met through photos on Facebook.

I'm filled with guilt as I watch my sister's blank, unenthused stare as my mother points to her father. I feel guilty because I'm hogging memories of both men; not only can I remember what it's like to hear, to smell, and to feel the warmth of my father's presence so vividly that even in the dark, I can recognize his name, but I can also vaguely trace the outlines of Faith's father. The cold clink of his metal chains in my palm is more than my sister will ever know.

60

"It'd be something different if you never knew him," my mother says as smoke and spit fly from her teeth. "But you knew him – you got attached and he *left!*"

Faith doesn't say anything. What could she say?

I still speak to my father every other day. We still spend summers together. I don't need to tell her that I have options – that I can always call my father and be three states away by tomorrow evening.

My mother begins to resent that I don't *need* her and her alone. She runs to psychics and murmurs that my father has cast a hex over me, she wants him held responsible for the growing divide between us. As we separate, my mother and sister nurture an exclusive bond.

In her therapy sessions, she says, "I'm all she has!" as I sit on the stiff sofa, crying. My mother grows to revel in the empty space in my sister's life, and makes her home in my sister's loneliness.

The first few days, I'm the only one who weeps. My mother and sister laugh as they try on clothes for the all-white funeral, as if dressing for a party. I want to shake them until the tears welling in my own eyes slide down their cheeks. The day before the funeral, Norman's sister comes to get Faith and for the first time, my sister meets her family. My mother refuses to go.

It takes my sister a week to register that he's gone. On the day after the funeral, I come home from school and find my sister cast across the couch, weeping. I hesitate to embrace her, memories of the man with color in his cheeks and gold on his neck dragging me back. I harbor these memories that aren't even mine; in the dark, I can recognize Norman's name.

In the dark, Faith can recognize Norman's blue, unresponsive face.

Idos y muertos olvidados presto, to men who are both dead and absent, there's nothing left. No coming back.

"I leave you with this trauma" reminds us that every story belongs to its characters differently, and often, the best narrators are haunted by more than just their own versions."

Destiny Perkins is a 17-year-old writer from Pittsburgh, Pennsylvania who will graduate from Pittsburgh CAPA 6-12 in 2019. She's also been published in *Creative Communication*'s 2013 anthology and the *2018 Ralph Munn Creative Writing Anthology.* She plans to pursue a career in art and writing in the future.

Maia Siegel

Community HS, Roanoke, VA

 2018 Claudia Ann Seaman Award Runner Up for Poetry

Because of the Pear

I tuck eggs in tomatoes,
their yolks pouring out at the touch.
I do not make salmon,
horseradish streaking its veins.
I stare at the 7pm light, blue on the snow.
but not at the white brick house down the street,
or the one with the small light-up tree.
I recite my lines for a play in which I say
No, mother.
I do not recite a word of any play
where I agree with my mother.
I cannot imagine birthing and dying
without crying clear snot
and it could have been the pear
instead of the apple for lunch today
that changed how I felt
about the blue light on the snow
and everything after.

Yes, so many times, yes. It's a strange suburban gothic; beautiful, chilling, and original.

At the Cat Show in the Valley View Holiday Inn

The judge presses blue ribbons
onto the metal bars of the cages,
telling the eight people sitting here
that a perfect Persian's head should look
like an orange
with the end chopped off.
He traces the eyes of a Cornish Rex,
shows us how they gently bisect
the line of the ear. *That's a thousand dollar
cat*, someone whispers.

Back in the waiting area,
the cages smell like shit and heated chicken.
The longhairs wear coffee filters around
their necks, and the owners drag their breathing
machines against their heels.

In the agility arena,
a cat lies down on the primary-colored
foam mat, closes his eyes, and sleeps.
Through the black wire protective barrier
we watch his white body lie silent
on the yellow foam square,
oblivious to all we go through –
our analog clocks
and our gas mileage and our need
for something to look at.

*I enter the dingy, fur-coated hotel with this narrator and watch – in vague,
self-indulgent amusement and terror – the oblivious cats being measured and
weighed against human standards of perfection. This poem jolts me effortlessly into
a guilty state of self-awareness, of human awareness, a state in which I question our
constant, perhaps inane search for standards, for something, always, to look at.*

Guest In-House Editor, Mikaela Ritchie

A Bottle of Zoloft Wins Never Have I Ever*

One of us is turning fifteen, and we are celebrating
in the attic, accumulating empty yellow Butterfinger wrappers.
One girl with dyed-red hair is drinking
soda with a Russian label as we play clockwise games
    in which we try to hide our love

of others' secrets. We keep the real bad ones
to our chests. The birthday girl, blonde with dark blue glasses,
    tosses a clear bottle of pastel pills
into our circle of cellophane sleeping bags.
She says she was saving them

up. And now my secrets,
that real bad dream I had once, those days
    I skipped dinner, are worth nothing
this round. I grab the pill bottle. I say we should
    flush them. Now, we should flush them now. She

doesn't want to. She waves the idea away and someone says
    that they've been kissed three times and my attention moves
    from the bottle on the beige carpeted floor
to their pink lips. The next morning I have oatmeal
    for breakfast and when I open the door

the cat runs out while I leave. I remember only later
the pills are still on the floor, next to the brown-streaked
    Butterfinger wrappers and Russian soda bottle, silent
    and chalky and maybe celebrating a little, the winners
    of the very last round.

* This poem is a Foyle commended poem from 2018

64

....

*From the second I saw it, I desperately hoped this piece deserved its title.
It's almost refreshing to read something that puts into words the dark underbelly
of the teenage experience. The matter-of-fact tone and purposeful use of
enjambment create an atmosphere that screams truth.*

Guest In-House Editor, Levi Todd

I Don't Care What Scientific American Says:

viruses are alive
in the way that seeds are alive in the way
that molecules pulse through palm leaves and French
textbooks and seedless clementines. I don't feel it
in my bones in the way Frank O'Hara hated orange
but I feel it in my blood cells,
scraped from bone marrow and still alive
in a way that atoms are,
which is to say
maybe not dead
which is to say
maybe when I die
it won't be completely dark and still
and something – not the heart, but maybe
a cherry seed I swallowed two weeks ago –
will still be pulsing.

. . . .

This piece pulses with a poignant energy of its own, buzzing with the unique voice and style of a mid-study session musing in the margin of a lab notebook.

65

Maia Siegel attends Community High School in Roanoke, Virginia. She graduates in 2021. Her poetry has appeared in *Cargoes*, the *Austin International Poetry Festival Youth Anthology*, and elsewhere. She was a Foyle Young Poets of the Year Award 2017 Commended Poet, and wrote a Solstice Prize for Young Writers 2017 Highly Commended Poem.

Derek Song

College Station HS, College Station, TX

Musings of Sunday Evening on a Pig Farm

my body is a broken temple:
i'm not sure when it was purified
but i can still remember the face

– doors closed – for Him.
he spent so many nights

i don't know

just on our knees.
i'm down here with you:

praying to find myself,
baptized. in all the ways
confirmed. to always
having *faith.* in *prayers*:

for everyone to worship but me.
i'm not sure i want to know.
of the priest who found my sacred
    body open
i temple. i holy. i spirit.   *sanctified.*
reading musings – forgetting most
    of the teachings.
if we're finding ourselves on
        kneeler pews or
but every time,
    listening to your musings,
        praying for ends in beginnings,
within a broken temple.
i didn't want it to happen.
remember.
please end   *– a man.*

The disconnect between the title and the disturbing breach of the sacred here will alter you.

Guest Editor, Alexandra Muck

Derek Song lives in College Station, Texas where he is a senior at College Station High School, class of 2019. He has been published in journals such as the Snapdragon Journal and participated in The Adroit Journal's selective Summer Mentorship program. In addition to poetry, he enjoys photography and music.

Ella Spungen

Packer Collegiate Institute, Brooklyn, NY

In a Sentimental Mood Reminiscent of the Rain

tumbling from a dark gray sky while you watch from beneath a
blanket of the same shade
and roll a mug between your palms, scalded,
almost.

it comes down so thick you can't see the new drops
as the older ones smear your window
as it creaks with the pressure of the notes that fall
on the pane.

this storm doesn't know you:
it isn't the flood you explored before
you are not quite dancing because of what your body didn't know,
but unfolding your limbs to reach
aching toward the open white sky as if you could touch the very
source of warm rain on a not-quite-summer afternoon.

no, the rain like tears, mixed with tears, is not in a sentimental
mood
because the cadence of its beats make its own song
that is not quite jazz but could be if it waited long enough.
it never does
or you never saw it happen that afternoon because you were not
dancing in your
own skin,
having peeled off layers
and stood clothed in only sodden lace and the silk of water

67

· · · · · · · · · ▶

draping in rivulets down your arms and the side of your wrist.
once it ran off the tips of your fingers
you found yourself cold.

summer rain never waits long enough;
unhooked from your body, it moved elsewhere
or finished, and you greeted the weaker sun with a self that was not
quite whole.

. . . .

I love it when a writer/poet rejects cliche. This one "makes its own song."

68

Ella Spungen is in the class of 2019 at Packer Collegiate Institute
in Brooklyn. She is the Editor-in-Chief of Packer's school
newspaper and the literary & art magazine. She has won several
Scholastic Writing Awards and a scholarship for creative writing
from her school. She is honored to be published in *Polyphony*!

Tess Buchanan

Pittsburgh Creative and Performing Arts School, Pittsburgh, PA

I Watch My Mother Sing Psalms in a Graveyard

only uses letters in *"Mad or puny, her wit cries for black graves."*

My mother wants to wake her grandfather with a tug of her black
      curls or an echo
of a eulogy. She keeps his obituary tucked in the passenger seat sun visor.

She wears heels to respect the dead, to puncture the earth encasing
their captive bodies, to pound litanies into their ephemeral flesh.

As we walk between heavy trunks she brushes decay from headstones
with each tear's shame, losing what's left of him behind her eyes,

dignity sobbing, rotting into wrinkles, turning the air rancid.
She knows she will cry: she shrouds each eyelash with a veil of mascara,

faces death like a brave fool. We approach his grave and familiar pain
reaches for her, sagging like swollen oak leaves. She welcomes it,
      says Come,

sit with me as I kneel, and tricks it into a prayer.
My mother crouches over her grandfather's grave

like a vulture over a body, hiding under ugly hunger
for his embrace and the solace of memory.

· · · · · · · · · ·➤

69

Her body is a stiff casing, a bishop's robes cast over stone,
and I stand behind her, presence throbbing in her peripheral,

a reminder that time has continued without him, leaving her
stooped, mud pressing through her tights to stain her knees.

- -

Such a delicate image of grief; I'm almost there, watching my mother pray.

Tess Buchanan is a senior at Pittsburgh Creative and Performing Arts High School, where she majors in Literary Arts. She has received a Scholastic Art and Writing Award Gold Key and an Honorable Mention in the Ralph Munn Writing Competition. Besides writing, Tess enjoys playing competitive frisbee and baking pies.

Ritika Pansare

Gross Pointe North HS, Gross Pointe Woods, MI

you

1. you are not the phoenix rising from scattered ashes, no, that would be far too easy. you are not fire that licks at the ankles of hope, the fire that lends itself to destruction so readily. instead, you are the rain tumbling from the sky & the floods & the storms, inescapable in their power, in their finality. the tsunamis that crumble entire shorelines away, like a match to paper. you may not have fire in your soul, you do not need fire, don't forget that thunder lies curled up in your rib cage, a dragon ready to strike.

2. revel in the wonder that is the universe, taste the moonlight seeping under your gums. & when your legs give out & your heart spills out of your chest & your bones splinter under their own weight, crawl home. bend & break & twist your own skeleton into stars & galaxies. write your own story & splash it across the heavens. & above all, remember, you are made of stardust dripping from the wings of angels.

3. & you are icarus throwing his arms out to the sky, wax scalding his flesh as he plummets into sweet, sweet oblivion. & you do not need to heed anyone's warnings, you are not anyone's saviour, do not wear their hopes & dreams like a burial shroud around your shoulders. live for yourself, live recklessly, let gold drip from your fingertips. &, isn't it better to have been singed by the sun than to have never flown at all?

....

Yes. An ode and a song of encouragement, this web of glorious imagery and classical allusions invites us to marvel at the galaxies of potential within us all. The tight, knit-together structure slices up the piece perfectly, and the ampersands punctuate the thoughts rhythmically. The more I read this poem, the more I fall in love with it.

71

Ritika Pansare will graduate in 2019 from Grosse Pointe North High School in Grosse Pointe, Michigan. When not writing or reading, she enjoys playing the piano. She is an active participant on her school's robotics team.

Lara Katz

Pierrepont School, Westport, CT

Optimist in the Smoke

Us kids don't look far past the rosy
Cracked lenses, only blushed cherries and sugared
Beignets for me. Tall Papa
Says he's a pessimist, gives him the right, I suppose, to
Stare blankly over our heads at the wallpaper peeling
From heat exposure, rolling
His own stained cigarettes.
All I have are spent
Matches and college brochures, a nod
To the hopeful future and an admission
To the past. We sometimes
Throw away Papa's cigarettes, swirling
Nicotine in the once-white
Ceramic bowl. I may have a sweet tooth but no need for Papa to
Be a black lung, hacking on his
Torn-up dreams and grinding his yellow teeth. Even if
His dream is self-destruction I have
Hope to save at least myself from the second-hand
Smoke.

*One of my favorites this year. Katz paints her story in shades of rosy
adolescence and shadowed adulthood, stained white paper and silver dreams.
Modest and poignant, "Optimist in the Smoke" is a piece that seeps literary artistry.*

72

Lara Katz is a high school sophomore at the Pierrepont School in
Westport, CT. Her writing has been published in *Teen Ink* and the
Bookends Review, in addition to being recognized by the Scholastic
Art and Writing Awards. When not writing, she is usually studying,
taking photos, or curling. She writes all kinds of words, but rarely any
concerning the real world, as the one inside her head is far more insistent.

Alia Shaukat

Liberal Arts and Science Academy, Austin, TX

Love Letter to Iowa City

Sometimes, after I shaved my legs, my skin would scatter with
tiny breaks, leaving red cuts to line my shins. I remember the sting
of it whenever I would wade into the ocean. I realize that this is a
specific sort of feeling, leaving blood-like memory like trout floating
in an upward confusion, dreams rising up through other dreams. I
wanted to give myself away like ragweed, strands of stem peeling
off in a methodical struggle. Longing, I would say, is a certain type of
remembering not easy to understand.

TO DO:
Finish reading "Meditation at Lagunitas" by Robert Hass
Buy hair dye for Ben (Olia in Dark Intense Auburn)
Get $$ from ATM
Laundry w/ Henry at 7
Question the reliability of our future(s)

I hurled myself across the country to brush back stretches
        of farmland like lint
to spit toothpaste in the sink and watch it seep into porcelain cracks
to write in a coffee shop that was populated solely by writers
to be told the difference between Big Bluestem, Sideoats Grama,
        Tall Dropseed, Indiangrass
to keep the bag of trail mix my mom gave me to eat on the plane on
my bedside table for the entirety of my stay,
and to tell her that I am not her little girl here,
I am girl,
putting face into ethereal beings
and allowing constellations to dot across my cheeks.

73

And now that I'm here, it's a sort of body missing body
as tears aren't nearly parent enough (we are contributing to reservoirs
      bigger than our heads)
never taught us that we should be like rings intertwined with other rings
instead of empty spaces between limbs.
CONCLUSION: Until we reverse the configuration of the umbrella's
bronchioles, force tiny metal snakes to scramble between stars instead
of raindrops, memories will remain hazy.

lastly, I would like to tell the city that she looks more beautiful
      while lying on her back,
more beautiful when we travel to the cemetery and see our dead
      swinging on the coat racks before us,
more beautiful when the Black Angel holds her wings above her head,
shielding her children from the rain that has already began to
      trickle down her own nose.

Shaukat's weaving of imagery, allusion, memory, and personal awakening into the odd
structure of a quasi-travelogue, quasi-love-letter makes for a breath of fresh air.

Alia Shaukat lives in Austin, Texas and is graduating from the
Liberal Arts and Science Academy in 2019. She is the commentary
editor for her school newspaper. She is also a member of her school
diversity council and a leader of the Minority Student Union of LASA.

Sophia Shelby

Perry Central HS, Leopold, IN

Train Wreck

I am lying in bed with my stomach rolling like the tide
It is two hours before my day starts but I already fear it
My stomach's shores come in and then run back into my throat
Making me hit the icy, villainous hard floor, awakening
Every part of my brain to its normal, anxious routine of thoughts
I run to the bathroom, clicking on the light too fast, and I am thrown into
A self-made galaxy, spinning orbs everywhere, I grab onto the sink
My pupils turning like binoculars into focus, my veins creaking to find the
Perfect balance except my feet take a turn then, not knowing which
Leg to support the most weight, but what is weight, really, when you can't
Eat anything because you're scared the smallest piece of food might
End up in your windpipe and cause you to fight for just one breath when
You really don't know if one breath is worth fighting for?
It's a toxic routine, making myself sick and fearing my bed
Because it only signals the bringing of a new day filled with new chances
To have to walk in front of new people, your own mind fixated on
The fact that they are watching you, when really no one is watching you
Because you can't even seem to look in the mirror without seeing
Your aging forehead from the countless moments you sit in
Your porcelain bones with your soul out in the backyard
Drying on the line and you try to figure out the best way to
Slide it back on even if it's still wet because you have a
Party to get to in fifteen minutes but you don't want to go because
You have social anxiety and if you mess up and they figure out you're
Nervous about just seeing the same old people for the one hundredth time
They'll ask you if you're suicidal and on antidepressants.
Which reminds me that I might as well have woken up two hours early anyway
Because I need to go to the kitchen and conquer my fear of swallowing
      pills so I can
Add to the rattling of words and fears of chemicals and fears of losing my parents

75

and lost Opportunities swelling up inside my stomach, which is probably why I
have a stomachache Which ended up not being the food I ate the night before
even though I worried about that for Two hours before I fell asleep last night
So after I lay in bed and find the courage to get up and coat myself like a pill with
Good mornings to my mother and Hey babe to my boyfriend I
       cleanse myself with
The lingering fumes of ancient, careless teenagers spilling out of my
       used textbooks
Wondering if they too stared at them with eyes that never close shut and
Minds that don't just stop working when you pull the dusty plug out of the
       electrical socket
My bones situate my flesh apart from my brain as I drift into the
Depths of my undesired passion for overthinking the next moments that will
Most likely never happen but just the one percent that I could start bleeding
All over the place just because I am a woman or bleeding just
Because I can't take it anymore is why I have to go to these imaginary
Trains of thought because they are so deceiving, making me gullible
Enough to think that each time I leave my own temple of nerves
Thin as a broke man's set of cards and cells as dry as the Sahara
I believe in my ceased-to-believing-heart that this time, just this very
Hundredth of a second in the history of all humankind that my very own
Dirt-based brain might concoct some way to get out of my fears and anxieties.
But then the bell rings, the alarm goes off, the microwave dings, the pastor
       says you are
Dismissed and I leave the imaginary, settle back into this rented home of flesh and
Carry on, as the star student, the athlete, the careless, young spirit that "I Am."

Train Wreck confirms what writing is at its essence: therapy for the overwhelmed mind.
The vivid, dizzy lines run in the same wild way the brain spirals. People my age need this poem.

Sophia Shelby is a God-fearing Christian who pursues God's
calling through the typing of keys into poetry. She attends Perry
Central High School in Leopold, Indiana, and is looking forward
to graduating in 2019. This young author finds strength through
sharing her story in hopes it makes the world less lonely.

Nadia Farjami

St. Margaret's Episcopal School, San Juan Capistrano, CA

By the Forkful

my mother's tongue was once sewn with
a fabric of Persian phrases,
but when her tasseled slippers sank
into American soil,
white fingers cracked open her jaw;
a crumpling walnut shell,

they force-fed her forkfuls of fractured freedom
and
trickled manufactured justice down her throat,
as if she were a
mossy faucet

and
now
she hums English melodies
as the whistling kettle sings,
wings of steam evaporating slowly

my mother,
a Persian girl,
masked underneath an
immigrant's blistered crown

If, as Jane Hirshfield says, all good poetry wrestles with meaning, here is a poet who digs everywhere and digs deep to equip herself for the fight. It's direct and unafraid, cared for and precise. This is not the last we'll hear of Nadia Farjami.

Nadia Farjami attends St. Margaret's Episcopal School in San Juan Capistrano, California (class of 2020). Nadia is a reader for *Polyphony Lit*, and her work has been recognized in the National Scholastic Art & Writing Awards, the Los Angeles Youth Poet Laureate contest, the Nancy Thorp Poetry Contest, and *GLUE Magazine*.

Ugonna Owoh

College of the Immaculate Conception, Enugu, Nigeria

Portrait of My Grandmother's Ghost

I paint my grandmother's ghost as a premature skin, peeling off to join the realm of her ancestors. I'm scared that she gets to visit me more to steal my words and pay me back for all the trouble I'd muzzled her into.

She once caught me in my room kissing a woman, her eyes a fierce fire caught between tubes of anger, her silence making me an enemy of myself, her shadow watching as I crafted my own holiness into hollowness. She pulled out a whip on my skin and crafted me into a rippled bruise.

My grandmother's ghost is a portrait of my solitude, remnant of this sceptic jealousy of my not coming with her. Not verging close to see the man on the cross. Rather, her ghost became a festered silent sore (or festered silence) stuck between my flesh and my bones.

Before she became a wilted corpse, she threatened me in a circle of fear, her words heavier for my heart to carry this burning flame of her lips.

She said, "I won't plead with the man on the cross for your rescue; you shall join the army of the beast, for your ears are broken buckets leaking the drops of information that seep into them."

Words were long lost in her bones that were her mother's lips, and she grew into a healthier seed, but since I have taken the world over the cross, my name, my soul would be lost from the book of eternal rejoicing.

I paint my grandmother's ghost as a heavy stone, shielded into a silent tomb. She told me that the dream of hell was real, that it felt like a tomb blessed with scourging fire and agony. But the day she died, her tongue became the scriptures of this dream. Like a scroll, it clumped itself into a spiral heath, her words a crafted template on her epitaph, my tears silent to wake her into being.

· · · · · · · · ▶

My grandmother's ghost is long lost with my grandfather's. She said it was better to meet love in the path of death than be a wreck. Maybe this goodbye became a liturgy of 'til death do us part. And her death is a new wedding taking these unending vows as they reunite in the afterlife, because her ghost is nimble, clothed in white while waiting for the sound of the trumpet to read the last wedding vows between this altar of her eulogy.

"Portrait of My Grandmother's Ghost" paints images – vivid, powerful and sincere – to show the complexities of human character.

Ugonna Owoh writes from a place unhidden in Southeastern Nigeria. His works have appeared in *Agbowo*, *Tales of the Tree*, and *101fiction*s. He attends College of the Immaculate Conception in Enugu, Nigeria, a secondary school for boys. He graduates in 2019.

Ekemini Nkanta

Brooklyn Technical HS, Brooklyn, NY

color you in

tonight, you'll be my sunset.
I'll melt you down
like gold
onto the horizon,
frame your body in stars,
an evening crown
too good for royalty.
I'll cast you
across heaven's canvas,
letting your rays

kiss the corners of the sky
until even the blind
are breathless.
your spectrum of lights
will fade to black
and we will leave
the world
weeping.

*It's concise and packed with imagery; it's tight and complete,
wrapped up in a cocoon of everything it needs to say.*

Here I Stand, a Masterpiece

people love to tell me
i overthink things.
that there wasn't a reason behind
all the times i couldn't find my
skin tone in the box of crayons, or
that when our teachers asked us to
"circle the thing that doesn't belong"
they weren't trying to *tell us something*.

so i listened to them.

when i was six
i colored my stick figures yellow instead
and when i was sixteen
i colored my body lighter with a
skin cream for dark spots,
tagged myself in posts like
"lightskins are winning,"
told myself i'd look
prettier as a mixed girl...
they never called us beautiful.

black girl curves don't fit cardboard cutouts.
we talk too much and too loud
they want us to lie down and
hold our breaths and
wait to be stepped on
as if Eric Garner wasn't enough for them
and believe me, i've *tried*
making my curls subdued to look like you
but my roots refuse to humble themselves.

so here i stand. a masterpiece.

· · · · · · · · · ▶

Ekemini Nkanta

"the best art comes from suffering"
so here i stand, a masterpiece
tortured artists slaved over me
so here i stand, a masterpiece
with a painted crown, i am royalty
body gold mistaken for poverty
we belong in
this thick skin
our handcrafted melanin
we are deities to be glorified
living temples to be worshipped in
and when they try to make you porcelain,
push back until they break because
your *black is art*
because when we mix paints,
black is the presence of all colors.

....

This is not only a voice that needs to be heard, but an absolutely beautiful poem. Finally, a piece that blends an important cry of social revolution with artistry and literary talent. From imagery to personal narrative, the piece excels.

82

Ekemini Nkanta is a dreamer in the "city that never sleeps."
She graduated from Brooklyn Technical High School
(Brooklyn, NY) in June 2018, and was named a National
Gold Medalist in the Scholastic Art & Writing Awards.
This fall, she'll design games at NYC College of Technology.

Sophie Feldman

Mercer Island HS, Mercer Island, WA

embrace.

open your eyes.

are you running away to
or running away from?

you've lost track of time.

is the sun going down
or is the sun coming up?

cool glass against your cheek
condensation a product of
your body at ease.

feel your head ache.
did you sleep with the smile
that numbs your face?

as you commit to waking
say hello to yourself
give your crowded mind space.

long drive
an arm touches yours on the left side
Passenger, have you ever felt so safe?

along for the ride
does this pavement atrophy
or lay itself beneath our tires?

the expanse is an embrace
a maple syrup sky
through a black frame.

this naked cloudlessness belongs to us

let's kick up dust and
freckle our skin
under the ever-present, once-forgotten sun.

don't stare out the rearview
welcome the static fuzz
that harmonizes with your hums.

pinky promise the taste
of chasing a million miles away
wrapped up in fear of the passing day.

pinky promise the taste
of gas station coffee
steeped in the water of an unmapped place.

pinky promise the
desert sand in the bottom of your backpack
and the remnants of coastline in your hair
and the pine needles on your picnic blanket
swear on the word home.

close your eyes.
are you running away to
or running away from?

. . . .

*Linguistically advanced and complex, it's short, sweet, and feels nice
on the tongue. What really got me is how it conveys confusion, relief, and a
bit of uneasiness along with the strange excitement of running away.*

84

Sophie Feldman is a singer-songwriter and poet from Seattle,
Washington. She graduated from Mercer Island High School in
June 2018 and is currently studying Songwriting and
Psychology at the University of Southern California. Her favorite
things are her family, fresh stationery, and chickpeas.

Adam Zhou

International School of Manila, Taguig City, Philippines

Dictations of the Great Mao

look deep inside the eyes
of the people who taught us
to bury the dead. you will see
a small clutch of plum blossoms
open like a fist. ground them. soak
them in water. pour this tea
for your nai nai. let it spill
across the table
down to her feet. you will drink
once the skin stops burning.
no cups. only hands marbled
with the blood of our flag.

This poem skillfully conveys the dark connection between seemingly distant political machinations and the lives of ordinary, real people. Through outwardly simple language, the poet elegantly delves into deeper thematic ideas.

85

Aromachology

Things I did after arriving in the night market:

1. Sketched out a mental pathway through the crowd of people and the food stalls, and the awkward unplanned placements of the osmanthus trees and the lamp posts, and my scattered train of thought.

2. Checked my phone for notifications.

3. Imagined the scene before my eyes in my next short story.

4. Hoped to see the stars amidst the smog.

5. Wondered what it would be like if I went back home now – another hour in the car that smelled like five-spice.

6. Looked back on my sister's stories of this place. Buying all the dimsum that could fit inside her crate, and the aromatic magic in the mixture of ginger, soy sauce, vinegar, and garlic. All for ten yuan.

7. Met an old family friend who couldn't stop talking about how time flies.

8. Listened to the faint song of an erhu in the distance. The Butterfly Lovers.

9. Pretended to know where I was going. The sketch of my footsteps the scattered musical notes and clefs. Rise and fall. Rise and fall again.

10. Caught the scent of a woman's take-out box and tracked the path to where she bought it.

11. Observed the row of pork buns on a table, their whiff – star anise and cinnamon which I didn't pay for in the end – steaming into my clothes. I would later rest my nose on my sleeve for more of the stolen smell.

12. Realized how each minute spent staring at a new vendor would be part of this chemistry, the lemongrass and the ground sesame seeds, the green tea…

13. Smiled. Thought about grandma's cooking and how I would always find myself getting stomach cramps because of how much I ate. All the family reunions and how Grandpa needed to know each ingredient to avoid his allergies. Wondered if I would ever understand how little I remember. All those memories in the air now, too, floating over and into the junctures of the earth.

· · · · · · · · ·▶

Adam Zhou

14. Also, upon leaving: considered the death of all those smells I've experienced. No coffin, no flowers, no mourners, no hole in the ground.

15. Hoped, though, that this was the new place of birth. And that later, among the planes I flew, the books I read, the houses, the cars, the dogs, the family I waved goodbye to – some form of a memory would seep out.

But in the semi-objective present, I walked in the middle of the road, taking that deep breath in. Accepting the emptiness. Feeling every ounce of it expand within me. Just in case.

....

I love the juxtaposition between the logic and order of lists and the smells and scenes – impossible to order – at the market. And how they all belong to memory.

Adam Zhou has been recognized by the Scholastic Art & Writing Awards as well as by multiple publications. He will graduate in 2020 from the International School Manila, where he has absorbed a wide array of cultural perspectives he aims to share through his writing.

Shridhar Athinarayanan
White Station HS, Memphis, TN

Amma: Americanized

at age 4,
I pressed my face into amma's hip and stated
hatred for her cooking,
repeated it until her supple sides
tightened
into vestiges,

but her hands kept moving.

every day,
basins of water pricked
by pungent spices pried my eyes open,
and festered and bubbled under my skin.
on summer afternoons,
gradients of watery orange,
laden with root vegetables,
awakened over a rumbling simmer,
their fiery fumes lifting to lick
my sugared nose.

every day,
I baked in tamarind,
and soaked in sun-suckling turmeric.
my bones stewed in spices,
until my fibrous marrow
was softened and infused with masala.
I stewed
until I was too pungent
for others to taste.

88

how I longed to be as simple as salt.

I couldn't understand her,
amma, in her tireless alchemy,
concocting reverberating calls to my ancestors
which I perceived as
hollow.
but as I aged,
and she withered,
her defenses blurred against
my militancy against leftovers,
against my pleas for peanut butter and jelly.

she gave in,
her palette now muddled
with creams and sugars,
the vibrant peppered *rasams* and *sambars*
dimmed,
the bronzed hues of her face flushed,
her sunlight-trickled skin
paled.

she took up office work,
and her once fertile figure
was now plowed over with
industrialization,
her body continuously compressed by
neatly-pressed pantsuits
and tar-black blazers.

· · · · · · · · ·▷

my mother, now,
is left
lost in translation,
from my cries that echo over
an abandoned tape replaying
Indian *shlokas*.

and amma,
burns away in her final kettle
of cardamom tea.

....

*This poem offers authentic insight into the imminent transition that many
immigrant children make through childhood. Through food, the speaker begins
to embrace a culture that pushes Amma away. "Amma: Americanized" highlights
this familiar experience fearlessly, unafraid of the unavoidable vulnerability.*

90

Shridhar Athinarayanan is a student at White Station
HS in Memphis, Tennessee. He will graduate in 2019.

Eugene Lee

Skyline HS, Ann Arbor, MI

three versions of the same silence

there are nights when you kneel beside the
river, wringing your hands until they become two
fists in glass: knuckles folding into glaciers.

the air still cripples with her name
the way a hush falls
over a wielded blade
but you feel her face dissolve
and reassemble when you spill
her name to strangers in half-sung hymns
not in accident but in undoing.

i.
in this version of the song
the doe is still wide-eyed and
licking the bullet holes.
when you call out to it, the
doe drowns – a flickering brush stroke
on the horizon.
the ground swells
afterward – wet grass bloating
to meet the silvering sky.

ii.
in this version of the song
you carve a trail of salt into your spine
in the shape of her face. no sound.
only the hum
of a motherless body close enough
to the surface for you to touch,

91

only you don't, because you're supposed to
carry on and
let her echo abate.

iii.
it was the night a shrill sonata played
like water spilling from the edge of a night stand.
same alabaster hands, same gasoline
river, same scattered lung but
in this version of the song you
swallowed the barrel and she disappeared
around the bullets.

. . . .

*Prepare to be stunned by this cohesive, artful poem. It's a lyrical, fluctuating
portrait of regret, three variations on the pain of memory. "Knuckles folding
into glaciers" is a chilling punch of permanence.*

Eugene Lee

Car Crash in Busan

here
your aunt says as
she points to a red dot on a
tea-stained map with the curved
point of her knuckle
Busan
your lips mimic hers
like a young calf with new &
glassblown legs but the way
you pronounce Busan with
the intensified B and
untucked A broadcasts
your Americaness
through the yellow highway
lights and your
grandfather's favorite
jazz cassette that has been
on repeat for the last half hour
you look up at
her again
the flecked
black hair the seawater eyes
the bodiless
pride in her posture
that you knew only
through the half
translated stories from your
mother of cigarette towns
and marinated plums and
shattered lunar new years
but all you can think
about as your head
whiplashes back into
a negative space is

how you can't understand a
thing she's screaming they
say when you're about to
die everything
slows down until
you can hear the
clock's metallic tic and whisper
one
last locked-lip prayer to
God but when you opened
your eyes the windshield
had already dissolved
into a thousand bullets
and bullet holes
and your aunt's faceless
syllables into silence
into a stir
into a crawl
into a hand on your
hand
and for some reason you could
understand the whispers
between her sobs
as she cradled
you in her arms
like a canary egg and
for some reason
you were not two
strangers
from different mother
countries lying on the wet asphalt,
an inch away from
the silvered mountains

. . . . ➤

Eugene Lee

on the outskirts
of the red dot
Busan
the fluorescent
lights
the gaping sky
her fingers

clenched in yours – more
than just
the same blood in
your veins
limning you into
coexistence

....

*"Car crash in Busan" is a wise and poetic exploration of
generation, cultural gaps, and the family ties that lie beneath. It glows
with confidence and voice. And what beautiful language.*

94

unread letters from a loveless generation IV

6:02

we saw it coming but kept
slow dancing to Frankie Valli in
my mother's burning apartment
our blood shivering & eyelids
drooping with consciousness i
started to taste the smoke

between your teeth as
my heart beat faster but
you see there is so much

i didn't tell you
about the mangrove organ
pipes & the autobiography of a
baiji & the woman in a
palm-sized photograph obeying
the laws of physics &
her brother who drowned
in gasoline

11:38

the last time your hand rested
on the nape of my neck we exhaled
from our eyes two transparent
    screams
rolling down our cheeks in quiet
prayer we dreamed
about the wildfires the bullet
holes brimming with answers
    the thin
screams of a stillbirth
the world we could not keep.

....

"Car crash in Busan" is a wise and poetic discussion of generation, cultural gaps, and family ties that lay beneath. It glows with confidence and voice. What beautiful language

Eugene Lee is a rising senior at Skyline High School in Ann Arbor, Michigan. Eugene has been recognized by the Scholastic Art & Writing Awards, Columbia College Chicago, and Albion College. Currently, she is interested in exploring the complexity of adolescence as well as the overlapping spaces between culture, emotion, and trauma.

Jillian Clasky

Northern Secondary School, Toronto, Canada

The Adoptee

Nighttime was liquor without the aftereffects;
it loosened our tongues,
pressed them into panes of glass
and dusted off the secrets.
I told you how I villainized
the walls of my body and you said
your demons were the walls of your home.

In darkness we wove myth from the mundane:
how you scraped your knees
on the pavement last summer and my mother
kissed the crimson away
and knit you a skin of bandages;
how I begged her to build you a bed
because you'd already painted a stain
on the air mattress
in the shape of your body;
how we wore lipstick made of cherry popsicles
and danced on my balcony
and you swore you felt your shoulder blades grow wings
from the places where broken glass and bottle caps and wild,
      gin-soaked fingers
had colonized the territory of your skin
and dyed it with indigo ink.

96

And when snow fell like a torrent of icing sugar
and we stuck out our tongues to taste it,
clinging to the lining of my winter coat:
twin larvae in a single cocoon.
The night sky bled like an oil spill
and at dawn it scabbed over and the rising sun
shrouded our skeletons in flesh.

*Vivid detail and imagery and a gorgeous weaving together of rhythm,
pace, and tone into a human, compassionate story.*

Jillian Clasky attends Northern Secondary School in Toronto,
Ontario (class of 2020). She won the Ontario Speaker's Award for
Youth Writers in 2015 and received an honourable mention in 2016,
and she will have a short story published in the Toronto Public
Library's 2018 Young Voices anthology. Along with writing and
reading, she loves art and can often be found drawing or painting.

Kaylin Moss

Wando HS, Mt. Pleasant, SC

We Are, America

I am, America.
My beauty glows.
I welcome the night,
a true reflection of my dark
radiance.

Owls:
convince them of my intelligence.
You bred me for servitude,
my serfdom bred wisdom.

Moon:
exhibit my strength.
Pull the tides with the force
    of my power.
I learned how to endure hell,
and taught my children the same.

Stars:
show them how I shine.
My skin absorbs the sun.
This curly hair is full, stunning.
Look at my wide eyes, twinkling.

I know you see me,
because you, you are a
    broken mirror.
You attempt to mimic my beauty.
Injecting lips, darkening skin,
widening hips.
Cracks, in the mirror.
Puddles, in the reflection.

We are, America.
You, are not us.

---

*"We Are, America" pulses with life: through direct pleas to owls, the moon,
and the stars, the poet insists on their humanity and dignity in a nation in
which other people are often unwilling to see those with darker skin as people,
too. We need this defiant refusal to be silent and submissive.*

Kaylin Moss graduated from Wando High School in Mount
Pleasant, SC, where she was an avid member of Wando's
National Honor Society, bee club, and various community service
organizations. Academic excellence, the preservation of the
environment, and helping her community succeed are her top priorities.

Riley Burke

C.K. McClatchy HS, Sacramento, CA

For Sacramento

I come from the flames of my undoing,
a lonely boat on many rivers seventeen summers back.
Buzzing, buzzing – the summer bugs buzz in the oaks on the bank.
Birds call on heat waves that wash over the river and
the trees and the grass.

To be shaped with the swathed heat of valleys.
To be forged in pits of almond orchards and tomato groves and
sweat from brows.
My home is a winter sun and a white sky summer.
A tree lined north with pavements that are wet.

A grid, pieces of puzzle put together by
The 5 and the 80 and the 99.
I rest on the levee and on
steady, mighty Freeport Boulevard.
Asphalt river, winding,
to my school, at three years old, one hundred years old.

Rivers entwine and entangle,
I nestle in its pocket, my rivers
The 5 and the 80 and the 99,
The American and
The Sacramento.

My valley is deep and I come from its
trees and streets and its sameness.
My home is here in the river, a buzzing bug in the summer,
      a lone bird's call.
My undoing,
My making.

....

*More things make us than break us, I think. Sacramento made this
speaker, who in return made this sensitive and reflective tribute to the concept
of home. It's a beautiful exchange. Broke my heart a little to see.*

Guest In-House Editor, Frani O'Toole

Riley Burke ('19) is a rising senior at C.K. McClatchy High School
in Sacramento, CA. She is the editor-in-chief of her school's
newspaper, *The Prospector.* She has been writing for as long
as she can remember. This is her first time being published.

Tavie Kittredge

Lincoln HS, Portland, OR

The Next Morning

Dawn drapes bed-headed trees
with ribbons of swirling gold
vivid against a world of shadows.
Glittering drops hang
in tattered webs and flattened ferns
and drip a second rain.
The storm's snores thundered
as mares trampled the night

Yet peace is borne on musty morning breath
sharp with cold and uptorn earth.
Birds whistle frantically again
surrounded by shipwrecked limbs
and fallen trunks
writhing with worms and drilling ants.

*Here all that glitters is indeed gold, yet in a way so natural that you forget
gold could ever stand for anything gaudy. I'd admire this poem forever.*

Guest In-House Editor, Frani O'Toole

Tavie Kittredge is a sixteen year old from Lincoln High
School in Portland, Oregon who hopes to graduate in 2020.
Her writing has also been published in *The Claremont Review,
Literary Arts' WITS anthology*, and she has received a Scholastic
Silver Key award for poetry. Besides writing, Tavie enjoys
backpacking, competitive debate, and cooking with her family.

Nicole Li

Shanghai American School, Shanghai, China

Heart

Felt

i blow out thirteen candles

and read about Montagues

   and Capulets

listen to Franz Liszt's

   Liebestraum –

dream of faerie lands

and moon-drenched whispers

Throb

here are a few truths:

the sun rises in the east,

  sets in the west

and your name on the tip of my

cherry-slicked tongue;

i will write a hymn out of it

Break

strung across the ancient

   vinyl couch

my spine is a curved apostrophe

a half-set of quotation marks –

i rearrange my hymn so

it becomes a threnody

Beat

shielded by a cage of razors

nestled amongst pillows of tissue

there, they say, lies

the crown jewel of the body

really though, it's just

some ventricles and valves

pumping in crooked harmony

I love the sing-songy simplicity of "Heart," and all of its
certainties and the uncertainties beneath.

102

Nicole Li is a rising junior who will graduate in 2020 from Shanghai
American School in Shanghai, China. She's an aficionado of felines,
terrible puns, and fantasy books. When not writing, she can be
found consuming copious amounts of bubble tea or bullet journaling.

Grady Trexler

Maggie L. Walker Governor's School, Richmond, VA

there are no kids at a funeral

and the little girl in front
of me grows up and grows
old before my eyes and
dies in one hundred
different ways, once
at the start and once
at the hymn and once
at the prayer, dying
spattered like blood
on white cotton
but tomorrow, or the
next day, or the next,
she will have to go back
to school and act like
she doesn't know
what happens next, like
they won't lower her
into the ground, like
they won't whisper her name
in hushed tones until no one
                    remembers.

. . . .

*It's a short, heartbreaking anthem for all the kids that were
forced to grow up too soon. The rapid-fire verse doesn't pull
punches, doesn't apologize for accusing death of snatching
youth. And perhaps accusing the adult mourners a little, too.*

103

Grady Trexler is a senior at Maggie L. Walker Governor's
School in Richmond, Virginia. He will graduate in 2019. In
addition to writing, Grady likes to listen to music and debate.
He currently uses a green and white toothbrush.

Ashira Shirali

The Shri Ram School, Gurgaon, India

Scents

A tall boundary wall snakes around Windsor Residency. The red bricks sit in a European-inspired, or rather, European-aspiring style. Inside the compound, rectangular structures of glass and polished wood rise from the earth. Large-leaved ferns spill at their sides, and pastel pots of cacti line the front.

Outside the brick lines, Sal trees tower and swathes of wild grass strain against the wall. A haphazard pile of tents looks as if it were dropped from a giant's hand. Faded clothes hang from wires.

A fat plastic pipe runs past this settlement, one end joined to Windsor Residency. Years ago, the pipe had been underground. It began to show its beige body as people and their cattle walked on the ground above it. Now, it lies exposed like a vein.

Shanaya Jaidev's family moved into Windsor Residency two years ago. Her father was transferred, and within a week, bags were packed, school admission papers processed and the flight boarded. She soon learnt that this locality sequestered in the forests of Assam is characterised by its scents. Within the walls, one can smell the roses that families hire gardeners to grow, perfumes that come in gold-embossed bottles, lasagne made from glossy-paged cookbooks. Outside, compost, the spicy oil of cooking poitabhat, the occasional musk of deer.

Every Sunday, the residents of Windsor Residency meet for brunch. Everyone attends – Mr Sharma, who moved here to undertake his latest writing project in the tranquillity of the forests; Jyoti, who sought refuge from Delhi's polluted air; Rajiv, the nature enthusiast, and the Purohits, who couldn't bear the thought of spending their retirement years in Mumbai's clamour.

This Sunday, Shanaya has helped arrange samosas on a silver tray her mother ordered from Japan. It has a raised rim with flowers engraved on it. The cardboard box it arrived in announced '10 times stronger!' "So you won't break it with your butter-fingers," Mrs Jaidev had told Shanaya.

In the garden, the neighbours' conversation carries along the breeze, as does the aroma of baked fish with thyme, steaming apple-cinnamon pie and spiced

......▶

mushrooms. But soon, one unwelcome odour begins to mingle with that of the spread. It creeps into the garden, attacking noses when people least expect it so that Rajiv makes quite an unfortunate face as Mr Purohit tells him about his years practising corporate law.

Everyone ignores it diligently until Jyoti says, "What is that strange smell?" And then they begin talking all at once.

"It smells like something rotten."

"Maybe a dead bison? Happened last year before Diwali."

"It must be coming from the slum outside," says Mr Sharma.

"I'll find out," offers Mr Jaidev, his face gathered in disgust like a mask Shanaya once wore on Halloween.

Mr Jaidev crosses from manicured lawn to forest ground. The smell intensifies as he walks. He reaches the small crowd that has formed ahead, and sees the sewer pipe that runs across the slum has burst. It looks like a mouth open in despair, with malodorous brown water gushing out, as if the pipe is as horrified at this occurrence as the residents of the area.

Mr Jaidev grasps at his limited knowledge of Assamese and asks, "When did the pipe burst?"

"This morning," a man dressed in a plaid shirt and worn black trousers answers.

A young girl with bright eyes hangs behind the man, running a stick along the ground and listening. Her hair is matted to an indeterminate colour and her feet are in blue slippers, flimsy and tattered. She looks away quickly when Mr Jaidev sees her.

"How did this happen? PVC pipes don't explode on themselves," Mr Jaidev informs the man.

"Atul's cart was stuck in the gap between the pipe and the ground. The pipe cracked when he pulled it out."

"Why didn't Atul go around?"

No one answers. Everyone, including Mr Jaidev, can see that the only way to and from the field is through the gap in the trees and across the pipe.

Mr Jaidev looks around. "Has anyone contacted the Municipal Corporation?" he says.

105

This question is also met with silence.

When Mr Jaidev goes home and makes the call himself, the clerk on the other end tells him that authorities cannot be sent to repair the pipe till next week as heavy rains in Guwahati have blocked all roads.

· · · · · · · · ▷

As the stink spreads, so does discontent. The smell creeps into all crevices – it hides in Jyoti's curtains and settles onto Rajiv's hammock. It wilts ferns and forces fish to swim upstream. It makes eyes water and people stay indoors.

Mr Jaidev walks back to the slum, Mr Sharma with him this time. They stomp through the undergrowth. When they reach the damaged pipe, Mr Jaidev searches for the gentleman he had conversed with the day before. He tells the man, whose name is Kishan, that the slum-dwellers must find a temporary solution for the leaking sewer.

Mr Sharma and Mr Jaidev cover their noses with their hands. The locals have tied cloths around the lower halves of their faces.

The girl Mr Jaidev saw earlier bends by the pipe, examining the gaping hole.

Kishan also glances at the pipe, which is still roaring with a seemingly unending supply of sewage, and says, "It is impossible."

"What do you mean?" Mr Sharma demands, his face purpling. "Find something to block the hole. Your people have broken it, after all."

"Cloth, tin sheets, branches have all failed." After a beat, Kishan adds, "The pipe transports your waste. Before these buildings came up, there was no pipe and no problem."

The conversation devolves into finger-shaking and streams of incoherent words. Mr Sharma ensures he has the final say by ordering, "Just fix it!" and then turning around and walking off, fighting the tangled roots at his feet.

Mr Jaidev relates the incidents of the day at the dinner table that night, forcefully spooning dal into his bowl. Shanaya looks down at her sock-clad feet. She chews on a carrot stick.

The next evening, when Shanaya is solving an exercise on quadratic equations, she sees a stranger standing in the garden from her window. It is the girl from the slum. Shanaya abandons her textbook and goes outside, taking a pollution mask she used to wear in Delhi. The girl looks at Shanaya as if it is her presence in the garden that is surprising.

"Hello," Shanaya says softly.

When the girl doesn't reply, she says, "Are you looking for someone?"

Through a mixture of Assamese and sign language, the girl says that she's looking for something to block the pipe. Shanaya offers to help. They search under the benches, in the greenhouse, in trees. They find a torn paper kite, a discarded rubber tyre, a dirty sneaker. The girl stays close behind Shanaya the whole time, eyes darting.

· · · · · · · · · ▸

Ashira Shirali   Polyphony Lit * 2018

As the sky melts into ultramarine, the girl rushes home. "Wait!" Shanaya calls after her. "What's your name?"

"Mala!" the girl shouts. She looks back once, then hurries on.

Shanaya goes home, too. The sweet tang of lemon muffins baking wafts through the kitchen. The silver tray stands on the counter, a doily spread on it.

That night, there is a storm. Daggers of rain crash against Shanaya's window. She thinks of the burst sewer, the dirty water getting diluted by the rain and percolating deeper into the soil. She thinks of the tray sitting in her dark kitchen.

Early next morning, when the sky is grey as a pigeon's wing, two girls stand at the boundary wall. A clumsy hand passes an object over. A firm hand catches it on the other side. They walk away in opposite directions, boots and slippers squelching in the mud.

When the residents on both sides of the wall wake up, they are surprised to note the absence of the foul odour. Mr Jaidev throws his curtains aside and sniffs appreciatively. Mr Sharma smiles genially in the direction of the slum. On the other side of the wall, Kishan looks at the stoppered pipe in wonder.

A round item has been pushed deep into the opening, a feat which would have taken considerable effort.

Peace and petrichor begin to spread throughout the community. The rain seems to have washed away the brewing ill-will. Slowly, the scents of the two communities begin to blend –fresh manure from the fields and curried river fish, clothes detergent and brewing coffee.

Later that morning, Mala's arms throb as she picks tea leaves, and Shanaya oversleeps and misses school, but they both have a glow in their hearts. Everyone finds themselves humming in the translucent morning; everyone except Mrs Jaidev perhaps, who discovers her muffins unceremoniously upturned onto a dinner plate, and her stainless-steel tray nowhere to be found.

. . . .

Shirali weaves difficult, funny, and touching threads with a subtlety beyond her age. Scents pulls you in with its sensory detail, and the flawed, vibrant characters, Shanaya, Mala, and Mr. Jaidev, who take the forms of people you interact with daily. A beautiful comment on life, struggle, and unity.

Ashira Shirali graduated from The Shri Ram School - Aravali, Gurgaon, Haryana, in 2018. Her stories have been shortlisted for the H. G. Wells Short Story Competition's junior prize and other contests. Her work has been published in *Hobart* (web) and elsewhere. She is a freshman at Princeton University.

107

Divya Venkatraman

St. Francis HS, Mountain View, CA

A Tired Defense

My mind is spinning and it rejects
This blank paper that stands still

You laugh at blindness, at those who keep their eyes closed. Here are statistics to prove that…the balance of probability lies…where is the proof? Proof, proof, everything is proof. You look around and see a world free of assumptions, but you have neglected to look under your feet. You are standing on one, poor sap! The assumption that the truth matters. Ahhh, you look at me and blink, or perhaps you become very red about the ears and start expostulating what the HELL do you mean truth doesn't…

What is truth and why does it matter? You say there is no heaven and no hell, no good and no bad…then why should there be Truth and Lie? Believe there is one truth that can be found if you wish…believe statistics are the way to get there…but please realize there is indeed that core belief, that *assumption*, at the root of it all. Blind faith is blind faith, and to find those free of it please direct yourself to the nearest asylum!

The devil of your truth-religion is delusion. But a) I cannot believe in your devil when I do not believe in your god and b) It is easier, simply easier, and I am tired. Goddamnit, something has to matter, one has to choose *something* to have faith in. And as far as I am concerned Truth is not satisfactory, not in a world where something can be a particle and a wave at the same time, not in a world where there are as many truths as there are people.

And it all leads back to the start, it is a circle, a snake eating its own tail. If capital-T Truth does not exist, then who cares if I, in my heart, believe in seas of milk or flowers falling from the sky? Who cares if divorce rates are skyrocketing; I can still believe in true love.

You worship Truth; I worship something else. Let us see who is the happier at the end of it. Sacrifice warmth upon Truth's altar; I will arrange flowers upon some god's. In the end we will both get up from mussed bed covers every morning and wince at our own sticky mouths, both clean our teeth with stale mint paste and traipse off to some niche in the world that we have scrabbled for ourselves. Pragmatism pragmatism pragmatism. It is our hands that matter, only our hands, only what dirt hides under our fingernails…my mind is a temple to my self and I decorate it how I wish.

108

I think you have to go deeper with this one. It starts in fragments of nonsense for a reason; as Venkatraman says, "there are as many truths as there are people." This poem knits religion and science and philosophy in a shrewd, quick-witted commentary on the futility of exclusive thinking.

The Pupil of Hafiz

Balancing on a shore of paper
I dipped my foot in a golden sea
Laughing merrily, it swallowed me whole
The gold bubbles in my lungs, my love
And streams sparkling from my eyes

I dance in a rain of wine
My feet are damp like the hem of my skirt
I caught the fever of happiness
While singing with the stars
And it is, oh, so contagious
So come and kiss me!

We'll squander eternity in a single night
Discovering each of the thousand ways to love.
Worry not. To take delight in the gifts of God
Is the highest form of prayer.
Forget, until dawn, the dry things of the world
Come! Let's make the moon jealous.

We'll murmur knowingly, wisely, sweetly
As we worship the miracles of warm skin
And memorize the fragrance of damp hair
Tell me, my old friend, oh beautiful stranger
To what better study could we devote our time?

*Through vibrant, dynamic imagery, Venkatraman shares her
exuberance and love of adventure. The Pupil of Hafiz seamlessly draws
inspiration from the past to create a powerful work in its own right.*

Alone on the High Meadow Trail

The wind is still sweet but bittering
A newly jilted bride, perhaps, or mint past its prime
My nose stings and runs, and I am glad to be alone.
The stains of crushed clover seep through cotton
Black, and machine washable, and nine dollars a pair.

The earth is reddish, cold, crumbly. I kneel.
Below me shimmers a defiant city
Bolstering a bleeding sun
That was first punctured at half-past-six with a subtle finger
Belonging to that which looms above me
Large, and dark, and assured.

I am small, and alone, and unworried
Weighed down only by an empty water bottle
And all the sunsets I did not see.

....

The first line of "Alone on the High Meadow Trail" describes it best: sweet but bittering.
Imagery mingles with a unique cadence to evoke a universally familiar awe of nature.

Divya Venkatraman graduated from Saint Francis H.S. in
Mountain View, California, in 2018. She teaches yoga,
practices Krav Maga, and enjoys cooking, dancing, sketching,
and long nighttime walks. She is the quintessential Jack: of
all trades, beanstalk-climber, who jumped over the candlestick,
and occasionally falling down and breaking her crown.

Gabrielle Broome
SAR HS, Riverdale, NY

Days

*//Saturday: his face is forbidden charcoal in my notebook, slumber, the
burden of couches//*

the afternoon air is too slick, bathing rented white walls in a coconut
drift of his breathing
he's sleeping in daylight because sun sparkles are melatonin,
drugging him with the restless lullabies of the imprisoned
my face, milky mirror reads it off woven like bandages, the sabbath
the laws in my face canal, I spit back at him.

dad's shut eyes are carved with birchwood,
lathered cucumber flesh, mumbling, a tradition
rising and falling
belly in his white t-shirt, crumpled like the screaming kite

time seeps in
the mug of evaporated coffee, the seltzer bottle
nestled in newspaper folds, sinking
lower, lower
into the pit of the window, your glasses
underneath strewn sneakers and empty bowls

you cling to today like him, like cantaloupe meat
burrowing into its slimy seeds, as that is all it knows.

. . . . / . . . . / . . . . / . . . .

*This piece dances between delicate and distinct, painting its picture in tints of white. You
come away from it calmed, and yet there's something else there – something darker that
you can't quite get to the root of – that sends you back to read it again and again.*

Gaby Broome is an artist and poet, intersecting visuals
with words though her performance art/video pieces. She
has received national recognition from the Scholastic Art and
Writing awards, New York Life Scholarship and YoungArts.
Her artwork has been shown at MoMA PS1, the Met, Plaxall
Gallery, the Art.Write.Now traveling exhibition, Teen Art Gallery, etc.
Gaby graduated from SAR High School, New York, NY in 2018.

Dante Kirkman

Palo Alto Senior High, Palo Alto, CA

Southern Dispatches: A Found Poem

(As briefly noted in the New York Times)

To-day at McRae, Georgia,
A deadly Blue Gum negro will be hanged—
The posse brought him to his fate in an iron cage.

The colored criminal has light-blue gums,
Thickly studded with short, sharp teeth.

Such a negro is held in universal awe and dread,
A bite from his teeth will poison his victim.

He declares that he will gladly meet death,
If he only has the privilege of killing Judge Smith.

And to-day at Mobile, Alabama, a Police Officer died —
From the poisoning bite of a known blue-gum negro.

The bitten man swelled up and never recovered from the shock,
Though but twenty-three and unusually strong and handsome.
For ten months he has been lingering between life and death.

········▶

THE DEADLY "BLUE GUM."

MOBILE, Ala., Sept. 25.—To-day Police Officer John King died from the effects of poisoning received from the bite of what is generally known as a "blue-gum" negro. Four years ago last February King arrested a negro, who resisted arrest and bit the officer in the hand. The arm and then the legs of the bitten man swelled up, and King was confined to his bed six months. When he emerged he was an aged man in appearance, though but twenty-three years old. He had been an unusually strong and handsome man. He never recovered from the shock.

For ten months he has been lingering between life and death. King's assailant was at the time of the assault described in the papers as a "blue-gum" negro.

This piece is based on public domain, historical *NY Times* content as a "found poem," published first at: https://www.nytimes. com/2017/06/21/learning/found-poem-favorite-southern-dispatches-briefly-noted.htm

It's a powerful, concise historical commentary with a relevant link to the racial oppression that persists in the United States today.

Dante Kirkman is a writer and artist from Palo Alto, California, where he is a member of the Class of 2020 at Palo Alto Senior High School. His work reflects his perspective on the human experience as a Black teenager coming of age in 21st century America.

Nora Paul

Oak Park and River Forest HS, Oak Park, IL

Smudge

One Sunday morning my father came home with an over-sized M&M tee shirt he had gotten from a yard sale. He gave it to me and said I would grow into it. He would bring pastries from the bakery near his house, empanadas and chocolate mice. When my birthday came around he would give me something special: for my 10th birthday, a keyboard, the next year, a CD player. These gifts were the manifestation of his creativity, packaged in gift wrap as much as tape with a landscape-scrawled card. When he lost his job in the spring the gifts became more sporadic. He brought in a yard sign that said "Home of an LHS Volleyball Player," though I didn't play volleyball. I left it in the back by the recycling; there was already so much stuff in my room. For my birthday there were scarves and red velvet cranberries, and one day that fall, a shattered cell phone he'd found. As I answered the door he pretended to be talking on it. He wore ten layers to my house in the winter because he walked everywhere; over coffee he peeled off his coat and sweaters like fingering apart newspaper pages. He warmed his hands on the radiator, and I could almost see steam rise.

One Sunday I heard him coming. I opened the door but he had stopped short of it. He was still for a moment, standing just a few feet away, and I wondered why. Later, he told me he had been standing back to get a fuller view; there was a little floater in his left eye that clouded his vision. He compared it to a speck of dust he couldn't get out. I thought I could see it if I looked close enough.

· · · · · · · · ▶

115

With the rhythm of the passing Sundays, the speck grew, taking over more and more of his sight. Every week he brought gifts, empanadas and chocolate mice, and it became warmer and the sun melted the chocolate on his way to my house and I wondered if he noticed but of course I didn't mind. I took the little bag, sappy warm on the inside and held my breath, looking at him as he stood back to get a fuller view.

....

This is a good one. It's hard to find a piece that can say so much without actually saying it, that has so much emotion bubbling beneath the surface. The subtleties are so small that you almost don't see them at first. The more times you read it, the richer it becomes.

116

Nora Paul is a senior at Oak Park and River Forest High School in Oak Park, Illinois. She participated in a creative writing program over the summer with The School of the New York Times, and her work has appeared in *Teen Ink Magazine*. Aside from writing, she also enjoys dance.

Krystal Yang

Basis Independent Silicon Valley, San Jose, CA

Buddha Jumps Over the Great Wall

The radio hums Frank Sinatra but all I hear
is the creaking of my grandma's orange fingers,
years of tiger balm ointment sleeping
in her nail beds, in her joints, in her white hair
like bleached bamboo shoots.
Steam from fo tiao qiang* melts into the smoky
sweat sliding down her face, melts into the sunlit
cliffs of her cheeks.
Scallops and sea cucumber swim
in the spaces between her teeth
and rice flour settles
in the wrinkles of her furrowed brow.
"Not same," she says to me. "Not same."

But it's Sunday and Sundays
are for school so I leave my grandma in the kitchen
and piety shoved under the doormat.

I trip over Converse shoelaces
to the McDonald's down the street. John and Sally
are already buying wontons and they pay the cashier
in green bucks with Ben Franklin and Confucius
carved between the creases.
I buy a bag of Hot Cheetos
and we plow through it with chopsticks,
red powder coating our yellowed lips as we joke
about how the school cafeteria
serves szechuan sauce instead of ketchup.
John offers us minty gum

117

- - - - - - - - >

and we blow bubbles until
our jaws are sore and our tongues go numb and we forget
how to speak Mandarin.

I forget to wear my slippers when I return
to John Mellencamp on the radio
and my grandma kneading taro and toadstools.
She's still wearing her qipao**,
the one my dad bought for her at Sears during Black Friday.
I squint at it and my grandma
squints back at me with unfamiliar crescents
and I think of getting her a new apron.
When I point out the glutinous slime coating the countertop,
my grandma tells me the Great Wall was built with sticky rice,
reinforced with the spiky shells of smelly durian. I ask her
if Buddha jumped over the Great Wall before,
and she shakes her head.
"Not same," she says. "Not same."

*Fo tiao qiang is a Chinese soup dish made from quail eggs, bamboo shoots,
shark fin, and other types of seafood. The name literally means "Buddha
Jumps Over the Wall."

**Qipao is a traditional Chinese gown first popularized during the Qing dynasty.

. . . .

*I was cruising through this poem until "John and Sally / are already buying
wontons" – then I sunk into a deep confusion I never want to exit. This poet melts
Chinese and American culture together so that the speaker's anxieties are my
own, and just when I think I have everything figured out, the final line sinks me again.*

Jessica Sommerville, Guest In-House Editor

Krystal Yang is a high school senior from BASIS Independent
Silicon Valley in San Jose, California. She will graduate in
2019. Krystal is an aspiring fiction and poetry writer, and when
she's not daydreaming, she's at the dance studio, baking
chocolate-chip cookies, or drinking green tea (unsweetened).

Britney Allen

Miami Arts Charter School, Miami, FL

Papá

Your faith has followed you far.
You slip into sermon
when your daughter's mouth hangs open
between swigs of beer.

Your schedule is etched in everything
you touch. The phone, ready for you at six-thirty
to check on your sister's condition.
Slowly you'll begin to forget
it's eating away at her end of the phone line.

Your chair is ready for you to ease into
at seven so you can watch the sun roll over the house.
You put the house on wheels so it will rock
not shake when earthquakes destroy the town.

You yell orders from the veranda and wait for them
to visit you again. You walk to church in your usual attire,
suspenders on your shoulders,
a hat on your head,
your heart on your sleeve.

YES. Small, everyday details come together to paint a portrait of a larger than life man. THIS is what we mean when we say showing instead of telling.

119

Britney Allen is a senior at Miami Arts Charter school, located in the heart of Wynwood Miami, FL, where creative writing is her art focus. She will graduate in June of 2019. Her work appears in nine literary magazines and several of her sweeter poems have appeared in cupcakes at Bunnie Cakes bakery.

Julian Riccobon

Pennsylvania Virtual Charter School, Pittsburgh, PA

 2018 Claudia Ann Seaman Award Runner Up for Fiction

Turtleboy

Chiseling

 half-born sea turtle glides across my son's torso, traversing skin and sea.

The chisel dances across my son's chest to shape the flowing fins, and Tama flinches with every tap. Grasping his hand, I flinch too, wishing I could wash away his pain like the tide sweeping debris from the beach, but Tama locks his pain behind gritted teeth.

When I got my own tattoo, it felt like kissing a volcano. The chisel was lava on my lips, carving *moko* patterns into me and reaping whimpers. No other lover could kiss so roughly. During my rite-of-passage, I was ready to prove my courage, ready to be accepted into the tribe. But my Tama is just a boy.

Once the turtle's head is formed, I can't bear it anymore. I block the tattooist's hand. "Please. That's enough."

But Tama gasps, the chisel hovering over his trembling chest. "I'm fine, Mother."

"No, love. You're not ready."

Now that the chisel has finished kissing Tama, a flock of boys gathers to gawk at the half-complete *moko* on Tama's tender-red skin. "Half-turtle," they snigger, and then scatter across the beach, cawing like seagulls. When I reach out to brush Tama's shoulder, he turns to face the ocean instead, folding his arms to hide his brand of shame.

"I'll never be part of the tribe now." Tama traces his tattooed spirals, pausing where the lines trail away. "I'm incomplete."

I trace my own *moko*, the patterns swirling across my lips like roiling waves. Like the ocean – beautiful but painful. There is still pain in Tama's eyes, even without the chisel digging into his chest.

· · · · · · · · · ·➤

Afterwards, Tama and I walk home along the beach, and Tama gazes out at the other boys splashing in the water. The boys laugh, and the men call to each other from their canoes, and Tama watches from a distance.

"Come along, Tama," I call. But he stops to stare.

"Mother, why won't you let me swim with the other boys?" Tama's glistening tide pools gaze up at me, so sorrowful that it rends my heart.

I wish I could let Tama join his friends in the water. But I know that if he crosses the shoreline, then the waves will reach out and drag him under, because he never learned how to swim. I never taught him. Because I can't bring myself to wade into the water, not after the ocean has stolen so much from me.

"You must keep your distance from the ocean, or she'll swallow you, Tama. I can't lose you, too."

I can still picture my husband, though the only witness to his final breath was the eye of the storm. I can see him silhouetted against the surging sky, his canoe tipping in the mighty swells. *Haere ra*, I whispered when he sailed away. Goodbye.

Now I pull Tama close and rub my nose against his. This is how we greet each other on the island. Rubbing noses is better than saying *Haere ra*. With our noses forming a bridge between us, Tama can see the tears welling in my eyes, and I can see his eyes still brim with curiosity, an insatiable thirst for saltwater.

That night, I float underwater. My dreams teem with turtles who swim swaying circles around me, but when I brush their shells they all drift away. "Come back!" I cry, but only bubbles pour out, and ocean pours in.

I burst awake to the thunder of my heart and the rustle of unsettled voices. Blinding light streams into the tribe's sleeping house, dancing on the warm earthen floor, but my heart turns cold at the sight of Tama's sleeping mat, empty beside me.

I stumble down to the beach, where I find two fishermen fighting the tide to drag a battered figure ashore. One man locks eyes with me. "I'm sorry, Aroha. He wanted to see the turtles."

With a gasp, I sink to the sand beside Tama. Pressing my lips to his clammy mouth, I pump my hands on his half-turtle, try to breathe life back into him, but Tama's lungs are no longer his. Now they're bursting with reefs and rainbowfish and treacherous trenches. How did you swallow the whole ocean, Tama? Did you even hold your breath, or just gulp it down?

121

No matter how I try to shield my boy now, he's beyond pain. No matter how hard I blow, my *moko* lips can't reclaim his lungs.

. . . . ▶

Julian Riccobon

The tides grasp at my toes, mocking me with their playful spray as I gaze seaward, waiting for a tide-tossed canoe, for a half-turtle to swim back to me. Why didn't I let Tama finish his turtle?

Now I'm being tattooed on the inside, the chisel digging grooves of grief into my heart.

Healing

After I got my *moko*, it took seasons for my scars to fade into intricate designs. Until they healed, I could only grit my teeth and wash my stinging flesh in saltwater to keep out infection.

When I kissed my Tama goodbye, I kissed another volcano. Now my lips are raw, and the saltwater only burns me more. Every time I glance over my shoulder, I see Tama sprinting across the sand. Then I look again. I see only glistening tide pools. Only a flock of gulls snapping at a mother sea turtle and her eggs.

A surge of anguish wells up inside me, and I snatch up a branch, slashing at the birds until they scatter. By the time their caws die away, the mother turtle slumps lifeless beside her eggs, all of them shattered but one.

Casting aside my weapon, I scoop up the mother turtle, now just an empty shell. And I scoop up the egg. Maybe an empty shell, or maybe with a glimmer of life inside. After I release the mother turtle into the sea, I clasp the egg in my palms, carrying it home.

Tama has swum back to me.

From that day on, the egg never leaves my side. I bundle it in flaxen cloth, sleep with it cupped in my palms, keep it near my hearth. Every morning, I brush my nose and *moko* chin against the shell to greet the baby turtle nestled inside.

When I wander the village, I cradle the egg. The fishermen, the weavers, the fire-stokers all stare, but as I drift past the gray-haired tattooist, he plants a hand on my shoulder. "I know you miss your Tama," he murmurs, "but that egg cannot replace him. You must let the tide wash away your pain."

"No." I hug the egg to my chest. "He needs me. He lost his mother before he was even born."

Suns and moons sail across the sky, but I hole up inside the sleeping house, curling around my turtleboy in a fetal position, whispering stories Tama never lived to hear. The egg listens.

Your father was beautiful, Tama. Beautiful but painful, with sun-sparkling eyes. I was only thirteen, the *moko* still fresh on my lips, but love clouded my mind like sea fog. I abandoned my home to marry him, but your father coasted away on the first tide, leaving me alone with you.

My tears speckle the egg, but I wipe away the saltwater. You're all I have left. You'll stay with me, won't you?

Won't you?

The tattooist is right – this isn't Tama. Just a hollow shell. A baby turtle slumbers inside, but he's only half-born. Only a mother turtle could breathe life into him, and I'm no turtle. I'm not even a mother anymore.

I drift into sleep, a canoe in the current, powerless and paddle-less. This time, there are no turtles.

When my dreams trickle away, I shift on the ground of the sleeping house. All around me, waves murmur and sleep weighs heavy on my eyelids. But my heart stops when I spot the constellation of shells strewn across Tama's empty sleeping mat.

My egg.

While I slumbered, my half-turtle must have slipped between my fingers and shattered. Woven fibers scrape my palms as I grope at the fragments with shaking hands.

Then, a distant splash, like newborn flippers slipping into the sea. Stumbling, I race down to the beach in time to see a trail of ripples chiseled across the water, drifting further away. I'm dying to plunge in after my half-turtle, but my feet stay rooted in the sand.

Don't worry, the ocean whispers. *I'll look after him.*

And for once, I trust her.

With one last glance at the fading ripples, I return to gather up the shells. It's painful, letting my baby swim away, but I must prove my courage. Closing my eyes, I press a smooth egg shard to the waves dancing across my lips.

"*Haere ra.*"

123

I love the layers of "tattooing" in Julian's story. The things we tattoo into our skin and the hauntings that are tattooed upon us without invitation.

Julian Riccobon

Assimilation

My hair is living proof of my past. Each twist in the locks is a challenge that I've faced, and each strand is a chain of ancestors trailing back to my roots. Every year, my braids grow longer, and every year I add another plait.

A pale warrior stands over me, wielding scissors as he attacks my head. The icy blades graze my scalp, and I close my eyes, wondering if they will slice all the way to the roots.

"Proper American men wear their hair short," the man says, as though my hair is an article of clothing, not a piece of me.

Salty streams trickle down my cheeks as my raven hair flutters to the floor, and when they hustle me from the room, I leave a trail of tears for the next boy to follow.

Now that my braids have been stolen, my hair will never grow back the same. But I still remember my roots.

When I was little, my hair used to flutter in the breeze as I sprinted across the plains. I loved running until my lungs begged for air and my heart thundered in my ears.

"You feel that rhythm in your chest?" Mother used to say. Whenever she held me close, I felt her heart drum-drum-drumming against mine. "It means you are alive," she said as our hearts performed a stomp-dance. "Dance to your drum, my little eagle. And never forget the beat."

So I danced and I lived and I searched for anything that made my drum beat faster. I climbed trees, clambering higher and higher until sticky sap glued my fingers together. If the trees had been tall enough, I would have climbed all the way to the stars.

Up in the branches, I felt like an eagle perched on top of the world, with the entire reservation sprawled before me. But no matter how hard I looked, I could not find my home.

Not the Indian Territory, but my real home. The land where my people had lived for centuries, before the white men had rounded us up like cattle and driven us westward. I had been so little when we lived there, but I still remember the whisper of a thousand cedar needles in the trees.

Out here on the plains, though, the trees were few and far between.

When I was in the treetops, only Mother could call me down. "Don't climb too high," she would sing. "You might love the branches, but remember your

Julian Riccobon

roots." And when I reached the ground, I'd tell her how I had seen everything from the top of the world, how I had watched the sun journey from east to west.

"Each direction has its own meaning," Mother told me once. "Wherever you turn, you will see something different. South means peace. North means danger. West is death. And East is victory." Here, Mother took a shaky breath, as if tasting East on the wind. "East is home."

One day, I told myself, "I'm going to walk home." And in my mind, it was that simple. We had walked from our old land to the Indian Territory, so I just needed to retrace our footsteps. It would be easy, like tracing a branch back to its trunk, or tracing my hair back to its roots. So I set out toward the rising sun.

But no matter how far I walked, I never got any closer to the horizon.

After trudging for hours, all I found was a weary-looking house with an old man hunched over the porch railing like an ancient eagle. The old man was facing eastward, his silver braids slumped over his shoulders.

He looked like me, but half-a-century older, and half-a-century sadder.

"You should turn back," the man said, his voice rusty. "There is nothing beyond the reservation now. Not for us." And when I saw the sorrow brimming in his eyes, I finally turned my back on the sun and headed home.

No, not home, I thought. Maybe I was trapped on the reservation, but it would never be my home.

A few winters later, I still was not any closer to the horizon.

Instead of climbing trees, I began to cut them down for firewood, to see us through the winter. Our house sheltered us from the bitter winds outside, but I hated being cooped up indoors. My muscles burned with a hunger to run, to climb, to escape my cage. All winter, I paced our house like a cougar while Mother watched from her chair by the fireplace.

She pretended that she didn't need the fire. But I still saw her shiver. Whenever she thought I wasn't looking, she huddled closer to the hearth, cupping her trembling hands over the flames. Every evening, I piled up more firewood for her.

"Come here, little eagle," Mother said finally. "I know you feel restless, but you must relax. Let me braid your hair." So I settled in front of her, and my hair flowed through her fingers as she folded the black river of my hair into little streams.

125

"I know things look bleak, but we can't give up hope. It's all we have left," Mother said. "Do you remember what we brought with us, when we left New Echota?"

. . . . ➤

"The sacred fire," I said. "The eternal flame." When our people lived in the East, we had kept a fire burning in our council house. A fire that we had used to light every hearth and warm every Cherokee home.

"When we left New Echota, we carried the coals with us," Mother said. "And we nursed the flame back to health. Even when our home is gone, the flame will still burn in our memories."

But the flame didn't burn as bright for me. I was only three years old when we left home, so my memory was watered down by time. I remembered tears freezing halfway down my cheeks and Mother's marching chant drumming in my mind. *We-are-Cherokee. We-are-Cherokee.*

"The West means death," Mother told me now. "But we must learn to live in the West. And you must learn to live with it the most."

"Why me?"

"They will come for you soon, just as they have come for the other boys. You must go to boarding school, a place where Cherokee children will learn to be like white settlers." Tying off my braid, Mother buried her face in my hair. "You will be gone a long time."

"But I can't leave," I said, my eyes flickering to the firewood. "Who will take care of you, if I'm gone?"

She didn't answer. Instead, she reached for her knife on the table, lifting it to her hair. For a heartbeat, Mother faltered, the silver blade pressed against her silver braid. Then she cut through the hair, her brow furrowed with anguish, as though she was severing a limb.

I gaped at Mother as she tied her hair into a loop and slipped it over my head. On the reservation, we only cut hair for funerals, to show grief for dead relatives.

But Mother was not mourning a lost life. She was mourning a lost way of life.

"I will be a sacred fire burning in your heart," Mother whispered as she tied the woven strand around my neck. "Whisper to my embers, and I will never be snuffed out."

I gave a solemn nod. Now that I was the fire-stoker, I couldn't forget.

But we must learn to live with death. That winter, the cold claimed my mother, sucking the air from her lungs in steamy puffs until her drum-drum-drum sputtered out.

It was only after her last heartbeat faded that I glanced back at the hearth and realized that I'd let the embers go dark.

· · · · · · · · · · ▶

As Mother predicted, the white men came for me later that year. They cut my hair. They burned my ribbon shirt and replaced it with a buttoned jacket. They herded me into a classroom with the other Cherokee boys, and started to kill my hope, one lesson at a time.

Forget your old names, the teacher tells us. You are now Jacob, Christopher, Richard…

Every time they call "Jacob" in roll call, I wait for Jacob to answer, until I realize that Jacob means me.

Kill the Indian, save the man. We must show you the path to heaven.

But heaven for me is the glow of sunrise, the rustle of cedar needles, the feeling of Mother's fingers in my hair.

If you speak your native tongue, you will be punished.

But Cherokee words tumble from my lips anyway. "I miss home," I say, and the teacher washes out my mouth with lye soap, like I've blurted a profanity. Maybe my language is a profanity now.

The second time, I don't care. When Cherokee words build up on my tongue, I stand up at my desk and let them pour out in a rushing stream. "I miss home. I miss my braids. I miss my mother." With shaking hands, I hold up the strand of hair that Mother had looped around my neck, the only memory that has not been snuffed out. "You can steal my land and my hair and my name. But you will never steal her from my heart, because her flame still burns in my memory. We are Cherokee."

But my moment of victory does not last long. Striding down the aisle, the teacher wrenches the lock of hair from my fingers. "All Indian charms are forbidden," he says.

"Please," I choke. "It's my mother's."

But the teacher shakes his head. "Trust me," he says, his voice rusty. "It's better to forget."

This time, they lock me in the classroom, sentencing me to hours of silence. As darkness creeps across the window, I huddle by the fireplace, cupping my palms to the feeble embers.

Isolation is a cruel punishment. There is nothing but my own voice bouncing off these blank walls. Cherokee words slip through my fingers, until my native tongue sounds foreign.

127

· · · · · · · · ·▷

"I am Cherokee," I whisper. The three words I still know. But even they are dying now, the drum fading with every beat. Maybe it is better to forget.

As I stare into the fire, my eyelids sticky with sleep, I think I hear a woman singing.

But that can't be right. I haven't heard singing in centuries. So I turn over and drift off to sleep, and I dream that I am an eagle with broken wings, crumpled on the forest floor. Every time I beat my wings, feathers flutter away on the breeze. Every time I open my beak, I can only croak three words.

I am American.

. . . .

All of Riccobon's submissions that I've read have been filled with a cultural richness and diversity that you don't find in the fingers of many young writers. This is well-concieved and well-written, and more importantly, a story that needs to be heard – the ugly history they don't teach, that shaped America and continues to play out today under different guises. A touching, personal,

Julian Riccobon lives in Pittsburgh, Pennsylvania, and he graduated with the class of 2018 at Pennsylvania Virtual Charter School. He has won first place in the Ralph Munn Creative Writing Contest, and he enjoys writing historical fiction. When he's not busy writing, he likes to tell himself to start writing.

Clio Hamilton

Lehman Alternative Community School, Ithaca, NY

 Winner of the 2018 Claudia Ann Seaman Award for Poetry

The Gender Dysphoria Sestina

Such a funny day to have a body.
This morning, I wake to a storm, but there's nothing –
just the chamber of my left ear echoing,
thunder and grey in the soft place
where sound finds skin.
I yawn and hear umbrellas close.

It's morning and my clothes
can't seem to hold my body –
instead this ritual of finding skin,
trying to see flesh where nothing
hangs; of folding, pressing, cloth in place
of limbs. Yawning, I look for echoes

of my tongue and find nothing. Echoes
of my feet, my elbows. I'm too close
to the storm now, trying to place
fingers and finding air. Can anybody
see me? Do I need someone
to see me? I'm sick of all this searching, all this skin.

From Mother, an answer: *you're sick*, plugged ear and raw skin,
yes, you're just sick she says and it echoes
through me. But still, these gaps where nothing

129

· · · · · · · · · ▶

should be? This clouded closing
of mouths and hands, this body
that doesn't want to play

nicely, this gap, this empty meat-sack? *Yes.* Place
a name onto this void where skin
should be, and that's enough? *A sick body*
is better than nothing. Yes. Her reply, an echo
through mist, and I find clothes.
A sick body is better than nothing.

My ear holds clouds where nothing
should be, and with cotton and mist in place
I walk softly, yawning at the day's open and close.
Sick isn't the right word, for this skin
and breath, but it's close enough to feel the echo
in stomach and mouth again. To have some kind of body.

Some kind of body is more than nothing,
even as I look for answers and find echoes in their place.
Such a funny day, to trade skin
for mist, to hold it close.

. . . .

This piece not only takes on a difficult form, but also a difficult topic, and yet
handles them masterfully. The picture it creates is of alienation from one's own
body, and it does so in a way that is both delicate and gripping. This is
really an incredible and relevant work, and I feel honored to have read it.

Drain

The day after Carrie Shimizu fell through the ice, she took a bath, though she was already clean. The nurses had rubbed layers of silt and shit away the night before; the gentlest nurse stayed with her in the shower to pull bits of lake from her hair and to shave a section behind her ear, where the hair had caught the ice on the way down and torn. The bald spot was the size of a quarter and red where a rope of strands had come out at the root. In the shower, Carrie had been busy breathing, but afterwards she'd tried to ask the nurses if she could keep it – like a souvenir, she'd said. The tuft was just curled in the shower drain like strands of clothesline. But no one answered. They had all been very quiet. They used warm white washcloths that looked like the bellies of fish, and hid them so her parents wouldn't see the blood. Which there wasn't much of.

Carrie knew she was already clean. She got out of bed the day after, and it was noon, so her parents must have let her sleep in. They were both being very nice.

When the gentle nurse had come up to Carrie as she was sitting with Mom and Mama, and had asked her if she'd meant to fall through the ice – *it's just procedure, sweetheart, we're required to know so we can connect you to a counselor if that's what you need.* Before Carrie could open her mouth, Mama had said, "of course not!" and Mom had said, "Our daughter is smarter than that, thank you." And that ended that,

And what could she have said? That it was an accident? To walk out on the ice after that thunderstorm, when the surface was pitted and translucent in places, like milk. To walk out on the ice after that morning, when she and Mom had been fighting over whether Carrie could buy a suit for prom. When Mom said they couldn't afford a tailor, anyway, and Carrie backed down and apologized, and Mom said, "You're so understanding, Carrie. Thank God you weren't a boy – I'd had enough of shouting and dumb decisions by the time I was your age." And Carrie said nothing; she didn't know how to say it made her feel – too small. Too quiet. And all tangled, like her arms and legs weren't in the right place. And Mom always said stuff like that, anyway. Like how glad she was that it was "just us ladies."

So, she finished her breakfast and said she was going for a walk, because Mama liked it when she got fresh air. She walked down to the lake and stood on the shore. The ice spread out farther than she could see, and the wind ran through her hair, and she stood looking out at the lake's surface wet and slick with yesterday's rain. It was so big, and she didn't know why but she wanted that bigness. Like maybe if she was a part of something that vast, she'd be able to forget how small she was. So she stepped onto the ice and kept walking until the lake swallowed her up. It wasn't an accident.

· · · · · · · · ·➤

Clio Hamilton

After the doctors told her parents that Carrie was okay – *just some scrapes and a sore throat from coughing water up. Some minor shaking in the limbs – just keep her warm* – they went home, and Carrie fell asleep stretched out in the dark of the back seat. When she opened her eyes, the shadow of Mama's headrest looked like a rectangular face staring down at her in the dark. She almost waved hello. But then Mama opened the door and Mom asked if she wanted to be carried inside like when she was little, and Carrie closed her eyes and said, yes, please. Mom was softer than she'd been before she transitioned, but the muscles in her arms still pressed into Carrie's side the same way. She smelled like oranges and a little bit like salt.

After Carrie got out of bed the day after, she found a note on the counter – Mama had gone to work and Mom to school, and Mama had left soup in the fridge for her. There was also a cartoon she had drawn of Carrie wrapped tight in a blanket, with hearts drawn around it. Cartoon Carrie looked like a burrito. She left the soup and stuck the drawing to the refrigerator door with a magnet. She went to the bathroom and turned on the fan so the steam wouldn't get at the paint as Mama said it would. She plugged the drain and ran the faucet. She took off her pajamas and the hospital socks, which were purple and had little sticky designs on their bottoms. She didn't look in the mirror. She could see her body fine; her nails were ragged from chewing, but worse from trying to crack the ice again. Her ears were cold and so were her hands.

The bathtub was half full and she put one foot in, then the other, and it stung as it always did. She was adjusting to the temperature, this happened every time. The warm and cold burned into her, but she sat down quickly. You're okay, she thought. It's just a bath, you dummy, and you have to do this. If you want to be clean you have to wash yourself. She reached for the shampoo, rubbed it into her hair as gently as she could manage. She touched the bald spot carefully. It felt soft. She rinsed and turned off the faucet and got the washcloth and soap and tried to clean herself, but had to rest after half her torso was done. Her arms grew tired. Her breathing was steady, but she had to look down for what felt like a minute until she could make out the rise and fall of her chest.

Carrie looked at her skin and thought about the time she found Mom's breast. She'd been in their room upstairs looking for quarters for the bake sale at school, and in the process of quietly opening the top dresser drawer, underneath their old sports bras, she saw it. It was round and soft, and her first absurd thought was that it was alive. But when she touched it, the surface caught at her finger like plastic wrap. It was cold, it was pink-brown and domed on one side. Sticky on the other. And maybe that was what did it, even though the thing was cold and didn't have a nipple and was sitting alone in the drawer. It was sticky, a few short hairs were caught in the skin and Carrie thought, oh – that's part of her. That goes up and down when she breathes.

·········➤

Clio Hamilton

Polyphony Lit * 2018

She touched her arm in the bath and dragged her finger down. The water was lukewarm by then, and there were tiny waves going along the surface because she was shivering and couldn't stop, her finger slid easily when it should have been catching like film stretched over leftovers in the fridge, and she thought of the lake and how her arms were empty and her legs were empty and all of her was soft and cold; her lungs sponge-light and she swore she could feel them crumpling; she tried for air and felt the lake clench around her throat in a gentle, giant fist. She tried for air and felt something tear through her chest, reaching up and up, but she was sinking, her cement stomach and ass against the tub's shell-smooth insides, trying to swallow her. The tub was too big and there was the awfulness, the scale of it: she fell into the lake, and couldn't feel the bottom. She reached her fingers and toes and teeth to try and grab something solid and all around her was water, and she shit herself. Like a baby. The lake is so old. She remembered: there was the lake, the silent aliveness of water watching her, and little Carrie floating in the midst of where she'd thought she wanted to be. Maybe that's what dying is, she thought. Being small.

Sometimes, Carrie does think that she died there. Not that a part of her died, like the baby in her, or the dumb teenager who hated how small she felt and tried to rage her way into something bigger, or the boy whose eyes she couldn't stand to see through because of how Mom might look at her. But that the whole of her was down there, lungs filled with the murky water that drains out from bathtubs and toilets and sinks. That they didn't break through the rest of the ice in time, and maybe the body had already sunk to the bottom or been eaten and expelled by one of those sturgeon they say are bigger than a person, and she was decomposing now, sitting on the muck and quiet of the lake floor, or hidden among the lake debris. Maybe some shrimpy, scuttling thing found her skull and was living inside it. That would be all right, she thinks. She'd like to keep something safe.

The day after Carrie Shimizu fell through the ice and kept falling, she got out of the bath and opened the drain. She was clean. Her skin was warm, and she dried off with a towel that looked like a towel. She used the toilet. She rubbed lotion into her chest, her elbows, and knees, and touched the new bald spot behind her ear.

The day after she fell, she sat on the floor of her closet and closed the door. The door had a handle on the inside, too. It had a little light on the ceiling and was warm inside, and dry. The floor was wood. It felt solid on her feet and she pressed against it. She put her hand flat against her chest and tried to breathe.

....

Parents often work out their own struggles with the "I want better for you" mantra. They think they can give their kids a better life by saving them from whatever their own struggles are, and often this ends up suppressing the child. I love how Drain plays out this common parental paradox in a super LGBTQ household while giving space for often-silenced voices, and showing how those voices are going through the same thing as the rest of us.

Clio Hamilton

After Eden

The magnolia outside my window
   blooms,
flowers soft and opening like lips.
I'd like to be as hungry
as a magnolia. As open as a
mouth.
Last Wednesday I sat, back
to the window and trying not
to look at the girl
whose eyes make me an onion
or an artichoke – some bitter thing
whose worth is only
in unwrapping.
I said I loved her.
What I meant was, I want to know
whether I want you or want
to crawl inside your mouth
   and curl
into your ribs
or have you peel away my
   vegetable skin and put
my heart against your tongue.
What I meant was, listen.
I don't know what I'm saying.
But my mouth is
open and outside the flowers
   are opening
too, baring their teeth.
Their petals already
extending, ready
to fall.

"I'd like to be as hungry as a magnolia." Lines like this make it clear to me that it is not a choice for some people to be poets. This one took me by the throat and swallowed me whole. Each deliberate word made me hunger for more.

Clio Hamilton, an Ithaca, NY native who graduated from the Lehman Alternative Community School in 2018, loves to write. She also loves roller derby, knitting socks, and trying to keep her houseplants alive. Her first word was "book," which explains a lot.

Jaidyn Lam

Seattle Academy, Seattle, WA

New Moons

Emering between waves,
sentience, manifest. Like
moss on rocks. In an urban
blink of an eye,

beautiful. As country stars. As
sunrise on steel kingdoms.
As tepid gods watch firework
    flashes
on the driveway, little flames dot

a sinuous timeline. Sit like
    a day-old
quarter of ham on rye on the
counter. Lazy and forgotten. In
favor of quivering candlelight

in the distance. Who cares.
The times signed in a corner store.
Heaven sent to So-Cal.
    Dust caught
on corners of citrus

sunbeams. Sordid and satin
seeds of a cycle, complex
    decadence.
Gathered messily by we who
can only see so much.

*The images here are subtle and sophisticated, playing off of each other
in fascinating ways; the emotions are perfectly pitched and build to a gorgeous
ending. While I was reading, my brain went, "AAH THIS IS SO GOOD."*

135

Jaidyn Lam is 17 years old and is not new to writing, but is
fairly new to poetry. She loves language and expressing herself
in all forms of writing, including essays, poems, prose, and
songs. She recently graduated from Seattle Academy and intends
to continue writing, academic and otherwise, in the future.

Michelle Cai

Adlai Stevenson HS, Lincolnshire, IL

This Dream

My father – who slept on a raft for a season,
who stacked cow shit
into the empty stove, who read
torn paperbacks by candlelight, who ran
barefoot until sixteen –
leans over between turds
and yells "Lotus root soup for dinner tonight!"
from the heated seat of his Japanese toilet,
as jets of water clean him, so that he
can use his hands
to watch a documentary
about his country
from a screen that
fits in his palm.

Over steaming bowls, as root
floats in thick slices,
so each bite loosens
more strands of silk sinew
that, instead of snapping, stretch
only longer, my father
says to my uncle,
Lotus root soup is something we only
could have eaten in our dreams,
and my father and my uncle
let wiry flecks of spit
escape through their
crooked teeth,

⋯⋯⋯▶

and they let their intestines gurgle
with loose excess
as laughter erupts
from the depths
of their soft bellies

. . . .

*I love the author's voice in this piece. Sharp, ironic, and visceral,
it offers an intriguing perspective on the American dream.*

Outside of reading and writing. **Michelle Cai** enjoys running
through the woods and working with her hands. A vocational
survey once recommended that she become the driver
of a concrete mixing truck. She is a member of the class of
2019 at Adlai E. Stevenson High School in Lincolnshire, IL.

Victoria Carl

Booker T. Washington Magnet School, Montgomery, AL

A Matter of Fact

I often sit silent as I eat, and I avoid eating with others; it seems too intimate an action for an audience. In this silence, my tally rose, whispering the damage of my bites. In its presence, dinner is a loathsome bother – the approach, the necessity. Such is the life of an overweight girl – I don't know any girl who doesn't suffer the calorie counting.

When did it start, this enduring consciousness of nutritional minutiae? Maybe the first time my Korean grandmother, from a culture where "Large" still means "Small," observed my delight at Christmas dinner. She prides herself on creating delicious food, succulent ribs with juice that runs down the chin and sticky white rice and fried egg rolls, carefully folded and bursting with special-made filling; but not for me, not for my mother. For Brother and Father, Grandfather and Uncle, who are big, strong, and celebrated for their deafening arguments at the table; their volume is a gift that shows their strength. As for me and mine, we sit on the edge, small talk passing from lips that do not open. Not for me...

I was maybe in fifth grade when I realized that if sound is silent, sight is supreme. Style – your style is who you are. For a while, I was *loose jeans, funny t-shirt*. Every day, that uniform: nothing too tight or too bright but I could still show the inside, where laughter and light and words abide. Then it shifted and actually was a uniform – white polo, navy pants – and the first day, I cried. I wore a skirt for the first time, and I loved it; the rulebook said I had to wear tights, too, even when the temperature climbed higher than my class average, so I did – only no one cared.

These memories are scattered, erratic; I can't tell the days apart. They blend, a shivering mass of *who am I?* If it's wrong to be heard, and wrong to be seen, then what comes next? Am I to allow any stranger to taste my Rosebud lip gloss; should anyone feel my soft, shaved skin? Some started then; others waited. I tried smell. I spent an afternoon in Bath and Body Works, looking for me in a bottle. I bought Love and Sunshine, Magic in the Air. I forget what I was wearing. I forget how old I was. I forget, sometimes, that that was me.

If at first the tally murmured *Sit down, shut up*, then next it was *Run more, eat less*. The golden age of eating disorders: seventh grade. This is the first time I really heard it. Before, its whispers drifted through my mind like smoke, but now – it knew what it was, even if I didn't. I remember my first gym class better than the birth of my younger brother. Charybdis had taken residence in my stomach, churning and swirling foam in place of acid. The door said five laps; I licked my lips, tasting roses, looked around at the empty gym, and started jogging. I enjoyed the first loop. It felt cleansing, pleasant, like a dip in the pool on an Alabama August afternoon. Then it turned fiery, and the pool became a boiling pot, but hellfire is inescapable; I kept running. It was only five laps, I told myself; it was only the first day. Forty minutes later, I stepped off their scale for the first time in my life, in all my five foot glory, and lamented my weight. (115 pounds? I needed to go on a diet. Those girls are 100 pounds. I'm fat.) Or was it my tally, quieter than air? I was 12.

I tried to diet like the other girls; they shrank every day and seemed liable to slip away in the breeze. At lunch, they munched on rice cakes and air, and called themselves stuffed – *So, so full; Gosh, I ate so much; I feel like Thanksgiving* – and smiled. I smiled back feebly, stared down at my full lunch tray and said nothing. One day someone – her name is lost but I recall dark hair, dark eyes – commented on how curvy I was. *You've got such curves!! I wish I could look like that, but I just can't eat but a bite or two at most meals. I wish I could be less skinny.* I can't remember their names or lives, but I do remember how she said curvy and how she said skinny. She sipped her styrofoam cup of water and I set my chocolate milk down.

No matter how I struggled, I made up for it at night. Each dreamlike episode seemed identical. I slept for an hour or three, then I'd wake up. I had to sleep with the lights on, so it would seem no time had passed, until I left the safety of my room and met with darkness. Darkness to hide the shame. I'd slip out of bed and pass silently by my brother's room. At the first touch of light, I'd slink back and repeat the process the next hour. Down the stairs and through the living room, where the time glared green at me. Through a single door – glance back, down the black abyss that ended in my father's room, to be sure the door was closed – then I had reached the kitchen; then I went through each cablnet and drawer, the pantry and fridge, and gather up whatever looked delicious and sometimes what didn't; I piled it all in my arms, and it accompanied me back to safety. There was never any left the next morning.

Despite my best efforts, I gained ten pounds every year. It became a surety; the start of school always saw another ten. 125. 135. 145. 155. 165. 175. Drawing closer and closer to the dreaded 200, when everyone agrees that you are obese. *You shouldn't eat that; you need to be more concerned about your health; do you have diabetes?* Small things are my only solace; my arms are muscular, I point out. I have a lot of muscle. My skirt size hasn't changed since tenth grade; I must not have gotten any bigger. I must not.

It has been thirteen months since the last nightmare, and six weeks since I heard the last tally. I'm not silent anymore. I may not be seen, but I will be heard...I am volatile, a volcano of LOUD and SOUND and HEAR ME. HEAR ME! Now I drown it out. And I tell everyone to do the same. Remind them you are real – not an image. A woman should be heard and seen and felt, and You have the right. Glassy eyes stare back at me and I ache to shake life back into them. As I clutch her sides, I realize – that's a mirror. I howl in her face anyway.

According to my Body Mass Index, I am Very Overweight; for my height, I should be 105-135 lbs, not 175. "Very Overweight." I wear a size 12, sometimes an 8, sometimes a 16. My waist measures 36 inches and my hips, roughly 38. I am Very Overweight. And I care, a lot. More than I should; more than I say I do. My friends are fit with slender waists and bodies they are proud of during the summer, when shorts are short and tops are narrow, and your skin is on display. I grin broadly, teasing their paleness, lauding my dark caramel, but it's just a diversion. They think I'm beautiful. I think they're beautiful. I think I'm okay. But beautiful doesn't exist at 175. This is why I yell – If I'm loud, they don't look. A woman is seen or heard or felt or tasted; we only exist in parts. This is why I scream. This is why I cry.

I yearn to change it all – myself and them. I treasure silence as much as words. I love to laugh, I love stupid humor, I love words, and I love to read. I love my friends and my family and my teachers, and I love school and learning and writing. There is nothing more exciting than the rush of understanding. There is nothing more exciting than the end of a new piece. It's when everything is broken down that it hurts, but I endure. It may always count, and I may always care – facts are facts, indeed, but I try to change myself. Not for me, though – for them: my sisters, my mothers, my aunts, my cousins. For my future daughters and granddaughters, and for my granddaughters' daughters and granddaughters. For the future 12-year-olds, I try.

140

The starting line hooked me, "I often sit silent as I eat, and I avoid eating
with others; it seems too intimate an action for an audience."
I often think of how & why a piece is as impactful as it is. There is honesty,
there is a reliability, this is what makes the piece really special for me.

The Definition of Insanity

It started in the 50s, our story of such pain
The world was out to get him, so he gave up his feint
Only twenty minutes, then thirteen lives are done,
It is a mental problem and not a gun one.

The University felt safe in this moment of stillness,
Until the Tower Sniper stockpiled his illness,
1966, another fourteen gone,
It is a mental problem and not a gun one.

"In rain, snow, or shine," they get your package to you;
Crazy Pat's giving gifts, for his mind has gone askew.
Fifteen minutes this time, fourteen lives and then he's done.
He had a mental problem and not a gun one.

Lunch at Luby's, today? Perhaps we'd better not.
I heard that Hennard's hurting, I think that I heard shots –
23 dead Texans, a state that loves its guns,
Trust me, it's a mental problem and not a gun one.

School like any other day, in 1999;
A test, a quiz, a paper due, time more to assign;
A journal full of targets, but that won't see it done –
Still, they had a mental problem, and not a gun one.

"Hush, now, my darling, be still, and please don't cry.
It's all a game, I promise, he'll only pass us by."
Twenty precious souls, that will never see the sun,
Somehow it was a mental problem and not a gun one.

The nightclub was asking, they said, to be destroyed that way
God's vengeance on those sinners should not be turned away
He struck down almost fifty, not quite fifty-one
It is a mental problem, not a gun one.

·········►

Victoria Carl

Paddock took advice from those who came before;
The Tower Shooter's room, his angle, and his hoard.
Mateen, your record's finished, Paddock had it blown
Oh, this mental problem is not a gun one.

One month and four days later, with barely time to breathe,
Another Texas shooting, as they lay down their wreaths.
This Christmas we'll be crying, but the country is not stunned.
This is a mental problem, and not a gun one.

Oh, look, another campus: Tech is burning, now.
A bully, a hat, and glasses; then pow, pow, pow –
Thirty-two! A record! And he'd only just begun,
It is a mental problem, and not a gun one.

Please, I beg you, please. Our president must know.
Spread the word to Congress, the community, your beau.
Thirty-five mass shootings in less than one-hundred one:
This is a gun problem, and not a mental one.

For a while, I couldn't get over the juxtaposition between the playful rhyme scheme and word choice and the serious topic. But maybe that's why it works. It catches you off-guard. The childlike writing of the poem reminds us that it is children who are being hurt, and the lighter tone mocks how we, as a country, refuse to treat gun violence issues seriously. And from the poet's copyright footnote, we see this was written in 2017 – before Parkland, before Santa Fe, before all of the horror this year has brought.

What Makes a Poet's Poems Pleasant?

Every breath is vital to a verse,
And each letter with care, selected. So
If I am – if the words do sound – quite terse,
It is a choice; for I cannot tiptoe

Around this fear: my words and I will fade.
Female, woman, senora, even she,
Do bow to male, stressed. Constricted brocade,
A fabricated jail: this girl in me.

Dickinson lives, though she begged she would die,
And Sappho dwells on Lesbos still, unworth
Blotting inky tears. Ask – who else could lie?
Women's words are without worth; since my birth

I have been told this, over and again:
For a girl, there is never hope to win.

....

So much of ars poetica tends toward the pretentious. But this is unique. It hides an important social commentary behind the frills of this sonnet's iambic pentameter. Carl declares she will no longer tiptoe around the harsh realities in her writing, and proceeds to lay out her fear of being trampled in the literary patriarchy eloquently and with great simplicity: "a fabricated jail: this girl in me."

Victoria Carl is a 2018 graduate of Booker T Washington Magnet High School in Montgomery, Alabama. She hopes to advocate for better education programs, in the U.S. and abroad, as a non-profit lawyer, before retiring to teach high school English and write a novel or two.

Grace Zhang

Princeton HS, Princeton, NJ

How to Not Say Regret

When karma shot him in
the bubble tea shop, they

shot you, too. Heart fell straight
out of your chest, plopped across

the bamboo floor, thrashing like a
fish in a net. Its ugly veins

rupturing, spitting ostensibly.
A desiccated, carved-out

hollow. Nightmares of
tapioca balls exiting the

revolver, ricocheting off
the walls, smearing all the

love letters you traced with
him in spilled sugar. How

to not burst while
rearranging burnt

bergamot orange and
darjeeling tea to call each other

honey. Now he bleeds
oolong like he used to

inhale it from your mouth
between shifts,

between the eternal spaces
where you didn't utter it

back.

Zhang captures how painful regret feels – how your whole body feels the consequence.

Grace Zhang is a member of Princeton High School's class of 2019 in Princeton, New Jersey. She is hungry to get out of the bubble and experience the world, hoping to study creative writing and computer science in college and someday intertwine the two fields. Her work has appeared in the *National Scholastic Art & Writing Awards*, *American High School Poets*, and *The Daphne Review*.

Averie Blue

Bentonville HS, Bentonville, AR

Summer Sorbet

I only saw her for a moment that summer, but I was hooked.

The swing of her skater skirt and click of her suede oxfords that only she could save from pretention. The sunset glittered through the distorted window and made a halo of her hijab.

But I could have sworn it was only me in that moment, staring at a stranger and imagining me next to her. Imagining me already knowing the flavor of cold confection she would order and saying, I've got this, in a way that would make her giggle because I was such a dork. Imagining me being her dork.

I wanted to stride up to the counter, just to see the face that teased my heart when I could only see flashes of a radiant smile. Suddenly, I understood why Romeo said Juliet was the sun. Even the painted backdrop of a starry night that shimmered on the back wall felt paled against her light.

I imagined the crushing beginning of a life in the span of a few moments between me and the girl behind the counter. I would stride across the linoleum and tell her my name, and she would smile and tell me hers, and I would tell her I wanted a scoop of _____ sorbet, and she would laugh at how I picked her favorite, and we would talk until deciding at 3am that plants had feelings, and maybe everyone in the line for sorbet had feelings, too.

I returned to reality when I was asked to choose between raspberry ice cream or raspberry sorbet. The choice was clear, and when I searched for her in the crowd – she was gone. But the warmth she had left wasn't.

When I lie in bed awake far too late, I crave that warmth only the manic pixie lesbian in my head could bring. To lie awake at night with the sun until the frosty rose tinted glass became a vivid shade of summer sorbet.

· · · · · · · · ·➤

145

From the author: Once again, I want to thank your wonderful staff for this opportunity and I look forward to my work perhaps giving other younger teens, who very much are like a younger me crushing on pretty college students at an ice cream shop, a source of representation or perhaps a moment of self-discovery. If anything, that was my biggest concern entering this process. That what the piece stood to represent would attempt to be censored in a passive manner for the convenient consumption of a straight audience. Falling into the realm of ambiguity is something LGBT+ people are very used to after all. So I greatly appreciate your openness to the subject matter and the acknowledgement that young LGBT+ people exist.

....

This piece has flair to it – the writing describing that first crush of love uses a combination of already established principles as well as quirkiness that gives the taste of the author's personality.

146

Averie Blue is a junior at Bentonville High School in Bentonville, Arkansas and is very much looking forward to graduating in 2020. She enjoyed reading and writing from an early point in life, spending many a pitiful recess reading *The Magic Treehouse*, but began taking it seriously in middle school.

Kaitlyn Von Behren

West Bend HS, Jackson, WI

daydreaming

we're sitting in an abandoned storage unit that smells
like my lungs look – the one with a red armchair spitting

out stuffing and a graffitied
eye popping out its socket, surveying
the first night of next summer.

you've snuck a bottle of something strong,
so we pass it back and forth, swatting
mosquitoes and readjusting on the duct-taped

couch, just a bit closer each time.
we're talking ex-lovers and dead friends and god
and your smile is wide

but it would still fit in between my hips –
not so long ago, you were a peachy-cheeked schoolboy

one town from me, a twelve-year-old
reading revelation (not knowing why
she plucked two of every flower).

. . . . ▶

147

now, we're passed out half-drunk
on a filthy couch under the stars, coughing
from dusty blankets and cannabis smoke,

but not so alone.

. . . .

This poem is a fantastic slice of teenagedom. I think that the lack of concreteness leads to a certain dreamy, nostalgic, and wholly adolescent feel. The author invites the reader into the piece as an accomplice of this moment without treating the reader as a stranger.

148

Kaitlyn Von Behren is an 18-year-old poet from Jackson, Wisconsin. A graduate of West Bend West High School, she will be studying English at Ripon College in autumn. Her poetry has been honored by *Teen Ink*, the *Scholastic Art and Writing Awards*, and *Button Poetry*.

Grace Tran

Westview HS, Portland, OR

Water + Sand

I. water

we ride on waves, flowing through dour seas
unseen, unnoticed, unwavering,
escape at our fingertips.
we are wanderers, searching for shells –
something empty to fill up with our
love, our hearts, our souls.

we bend, twisting our limbs
like magic. we fight our way past
invisible walls, one eye behind our backs
and the thought that we are our own people. we
answer to ourselves with our heads
held high. we are
who we made ourselves.

we are words rolling off our tongues, foreign even to
    the cleverest ear and we are
food laced with unknown tastes that remind us of home
and a place we are not sure will ever welcome us back.
there is a melancholy heartache with every meal, three
placemats for family and one for the country
we left behind.

we flew here on the backs of angels, hiding our fears
    behind tight lips and our wide, uncertain eyes. we left our homes to
        belong in some place we didn't understand,
     contorting our bodies, our minds, our beliefs to walk the streets
     of a place we begged to accept us.

149

we are deciding what can be ours, deciding what is a big
dream and what is small
and we are not knowing where we are going
but knowing that we will get there. we are hopes and ambitions and
picturing what can be and what will be.
we are shapeshifters, and we move
like water.

II. sand

we gave up our home for a place where dreams were
hidden behind walls painted white, every
step into a new direction, an unexplored frontier. we
sank, anchored to the bottom
of the ocean, pulled down by the currents
that rooted us to a home that was no longer home.
they promised our names in lights, flashing
above the cityscapes, whispered of things we could
never have dreamed of. we were
moored to a boat that drifted further and further
from the lights we knew
to the ones we could not see.

it was the eve of magic things, a sprinkle of
fairy dust to cast us away, birds of the night, ascending through
the bitter air. we feared the fall, the
icarian myth, to stay aloft
half between heaven and earth
unsure
of whether our feet would stand when we reached
the ground again.

some of us walk on water, a light kiss
but others do not;
perhaps we sink, but there we stay
to rise up to the surface, someday, somewhere,

·········➤

Polyphony Lit * 2018

from the ocean depths to the surface where
    the waves can distort and twist our faces
or mold them into something we are not.

we are the millions of grains that
sift through the waves and we are
making our way to the shore.

. . . .

I love the gentle ebb and flow of the poem. The mixed tides of
emotions that come with immigration wash over you, building
empathy that is so lacking in the current political situation.

151

Grace Tran attends Westview High School in Portland, Oregon
and will graduate in 2019. She was "Best of Issue" winner of the
American High School Poets "Just Poetry" quarterly contest.

Isabella Jiang

Cresskill HS, Cresskill, NJ

Hua Ren

I. Supermarket

Jackfruit can kill / if dropped off a thirty-foot ledge.

Here death reeks of sauce refried, its red hands rubber-banded /
shut. Marinated, two birds rotate / on black wire. Geese painted
/ in peanut sauce. I used to squat / by the row of tanks at the
back, to glimpse / the big sea bass, / the angry crab, the
unmoving toad. / Now I won't meet their shiny eyes, instead

scour the shelves / for crispy water chestnuts, cool sacks of rice.
I race past twelve brands of soybean drink / and a soft murmur

of Free sample, free / sample. Ginseng to heal / and warm the
feet. Sesame / to blacken the hair. Nearly slip / on
wonton wrappers / plastered across the speckled tiles.

A basket of fried dough sits in the butcher's air. I reach; Mama /
says no, it's not for / free. Sales technique: Touch it / to pay for
it. Get the cheaper soy and we'll go.

II. Cafeteria

I break a bone- / china bowl.

A treacherous realm. Friends / murmur of skin cream and faulty eyelid
/ surgery, exchange scores / from the sides of our mouths. My face
cracks / like the deep-fried skin of the peking duck: yellow-fleshed,
/ gossamer-thin. We eat to grow tall / and stay petite. My lunch is
never stolen.

·········➤

III. Home

If you dry your laundry on the clothesline / it will smell like the sun.

Chinese celery is flimsier but it has a sharper, more pungent
taste / Mama says, / boiling the sweet ginger soup. We gulp hot
tea / before it becomes / bearable; swallow / fungi like black
silks. Fungi / cleans the brain. Carrots, / the vision.

Over the clatter / of china, Mama / tells me of communism:
Yeye fought for Nam. Eat fisheyes / and your eyes will shine too. I /
am crying / silently because I didn't get an / A and Nainai didn't get
/ an education. Yeye is turning / seventy-seven and we eat / tangmian
for a long life. He who does not clean his plate / cleans the dishes.

*"Hua Ren" breaks beyond convention and somehow, despite its
singularity, drenches the reader in universal nostalgia.*

153

Isabella Jiang is a member of the class of 2020 at
Cresskill HS in Cresskill, NJ. Her work appears in *Tahoma
Literary Review*, *The Underscore Review*, and *The Jenny
Magazine*. Her poetry has previously been recognized by the
Alliance for Young Artists and Writers and The Poetry Society.

Dana Dykiel

Acton-Boxborough Regional HS, Acton, MA

 2018 Claudia Ann Seaman Award Runner Up for Creative Nonfiction

Ambiguous Truths

We take the train to Boston, and pretend the City is ours. We hold our hands above our heads and see our fingers as skyscrapers, clawing at the sun. The City is our heaven, cast in stone and winding streets; we model ourselves from it, but we are not glass and steel and concrete, we are skin and bones and weak willpower, and we crumble with the bricks and dirt and old snow turned to sludge.

On the way home we are tired, and more aware than ever of our disillusionment. Still, we hold the City in our hearts, and hope grows through arteries and valves like plants through cracks of the sidewalk. We think we will grow older, *we will be happy one day, we will drink coffee in the City and it will taste like ambrosia.*

The thought is ridiculous and immature. I scorn it as much as I believe it.

I ask my friend, a few days later, "Is it still deception if you're self-aware?"

She replies, "Is it necessary to deceive yourself to keep moving forward?"

She doesn't answer my question directly, but she asks a more important one I didn't consider. In my bedroom, I absorb the signs of my unreality; the silver-tinted sunlight that tastes like licorice, cold and sweet against the sky-blue walls, adorning my paintings and sketches with an aching nostalgia. This room is mine, and mine alone. I keep it stark, organized with a systematic purpose. I believe that anyone could walk inside and understand everything there is to know about me, if only the objects could communicate their stories, if only I could turn light into sound and sound into music and music into feeling to explain why early-morning sunlight is the most beautiful thing I could hope to describe.

I have always seen myself as fog, something sweeping and malleable. It is in these quiet moments I realize I have filled this room, this little town I call home, and condensed around it like drops of water. The city has lost its visceral sharpness, and as I run my hand along the glass and steel of the train window,

.... ➤

for the first time it feels soft. I realize I have found a place for myself in the blue sunlight; I realize I could be happy anywhere.

We drink coffee in the city, and the liquid feels golden, molten. Yet it is not heaven. It is real, and in that moment, as with every moment, I have never felt more alive.

I tell my friend, in low tones, that I have changed.

She asks if I am deceiving myself. "It's still romanticism," she says. "All you've done is found a different truth."

"Yes," I answer, "But it's *mine*."

She sips her drink, her eyes deep and thoughtful. I am struck by the thought that she is beautiful; that I will never completely understand why, that I will never find her truth, that she will find her heaven without me, because the one we searched for together was of false promises. Yet we will try to reach each other over this small, round table; we will try to understand each other, we will string our words like jewels and offer our sentences like necklaces in hopes the other will appreciate their worth, in hopes that we will share a small piece of our ambiguous truths. And that is enough.

***

I take the train to the city and know the world is mine. I hold my hands above my head and feel the sun, warm and welcoming in my palms. My skin and bones are cast in stone and winding streets, in fields and country roads, in crisp blue bedrooms; and as I stand tall among the bricks and dirt, I find beauty in the old snow turned to sludge.

A beautiful love letter to a city that has transformed Dykiel. The ease of his prose envelops me and transports me to this almost ethereal city. Dykiel tackles the broad idea of existentialism with ease and eloquence, incorporating details that enrich the experience in a way that ebbs and flows and builds.

155

Dana Dykiel

Dana Dykiel

Acton-Boxborough Regional HS, Acton, MA

What You Don't Know

I want to tell you that the subway map
Looks like a disembodied heart, with colored lines
Spilling blood from broken vessels. You should know
The fog from the city has not left since this morning,
And by now it must have sunk deep enough
To become a part of me; I am not the only one
Who has seen the cold mist beneath their skin,
Reflected over walls of rolling brick. An image,
Disconnected from everyone and everything.

I am among those who wonder
If love is salvation or self-destruction:
If it takes more bravery to say "I love you"
Or "I'm leaving you", and if either
Is tantamount to suicide.

Darling, this story has been told too many times

And they had to cut the locks from the couple's bridge in Paris
Because the weight was too heavy to bear; we know better
Than to hope for forever. We have traded our locks
 For copper coins, and cast them in the river below.
We wait for a splash of water and not a clang
Of discordant metal from those who came before, yet

· · · · · · · · · ➤

I still hear the reerberations of their oaths
As I ride this empty subway car. A part of me
Cannot help but believe this story will end the same way

Even if it is you and I who tell it.

. . . .

This isn't your ordinary love poem. It doesn't promise forevers, but something almost more beautiful—swapping locks for coins and knowing that love is finite but trying anyway. It's real, it's raw, and it doesn't pretend that love is anything that it's not.

157

While a student at Acton-Boxborough Regional High School, class of 2018, **Dana Dykiel** worked as an editor for *Polyphony Lit* and *Window Seat Magazine*. His own work has appeared in publications such as the *Blue Marble Review* and *Kingdoms in the Wild*. To keep up with Dana's current projects, visit danadykiel.wordpress.com.

Dana Dykiel

Kathleen Noren

New Trier HS, Winnetka, IL

Home

I turn fifteen tomorrow, but somehow at Grandma's, I feel like I'm seven years old again, stuffing s'mores into my chubby, chocolate-covered cheeks. I bite into the burnt marshmallow sandwiched between a cold block of Hershey's chocolate and two stale halves of a graham cracker. The taste is sweet, yet bitter, like Grandma's pumpkin pie on Thanksgiving, except it's not Thanksgiving, and instead of a warm, flaky crust, there's a coat of ash with a pinch of dirt. The marshmallow sticks to my fingers; perfect for catching fireflies. The bark from the twig makes my hands feel rough, like two pieces of sandpaper with thumbs. The smoke scorches my eyes, yet there's nothing sweeter than the smell of a handmade fire...and a hint of bug spray.

Stars like this only shine in Coloma. There's something about the way they crowd each other like the freckles on Patrick's face. I savor every "pheeeeeeeew...BOOM!...hsssssssssss" I hear from Martha's house across the lake, as I watch the light of the fireworks trickle, then dissolve like the sparklers my brother puts in his mouth, pretending he's a dragon. We laugh, because we know we won't see Danny like this until next year at Grandma's. Not as long as he's at work, and Maggie's in New York, and Mary Claire's at her friend's house, and Will and Emily and are in New Jersey, and Ashley's in Wisconsin, and Lauren's at college, and Megan's still in med school, and Ryan has a swim meet, and Quinn has a golf tournament, and Peter has a football game, and Uncle Paul's working, and so is my dad, and so is Kelly's dad, and so is Charlie's dad.

Not tonight. Tonight, I look around and I don't see a puzzle full of missing pieces; I see a picture. A picture I wish I could put in a gold frame and lay flat on the ceiling above my bed, so every night when I go to sleep I can relive the piercing sound of Martha's fireworks and the bittersweet taste of a homemade s'more, watching freckle-like stars illuminate the dark sky, getting to know the mighty dragon my brother keeps locked up in his dungeon all year. Because they say it's harder to fall asleep when you're away from home.

158

At the end of the night, I nestle myself in one of Grandma's handmade quilts, burying my feet in the cold sand, trying to resist the urge to itch my mosquito bites. I listen to the fire crackle and snooze to the serene sound of waves crashing. My eyes are closed, but I still feel at ease because tonight, I'm seven years old and I don't have to look at the picture frame to know it isn't crooked. That's when I know I'm home.

What I like most about this piece is the simple retrospective of a young person looking back at their even younger self – at the not-quite-perfect home that somehow still feels perfect.

Kathleen Noren is a senior at New Trier High School in Winnetka, Illinois. When her sophomore English teacher submitted an old writing assignment without her knowledge to a school literary magazine, *Logos*, in 2018, she was inspired to enter her piece in *Polyphony Lit.*

Lauren James

Goose Creek HS, Goose Creek, SC

a confession

in the fog of purgatory beach,
you draw your sins in the sand because you know
the tide will come in, wash the earth clean
of your decisions, and leave behind a promise of
heaven.

soon after, the water retreats before you can feel it
run over your fingers; each side of the horizon is
as grey as the ground on which you walk blindly
toward a vague sound that people say is the ocean,
tainting the smooth sand with your forbidden footprints.
some time ago, it was written that one should know what
the ocean feels like without having to touch it.

you look back at the disheveled sand behind you; what was
once beautiful is now marked with jagged craters of
your seemingly infinite mistakes.
but you remember the pattern of the tide, find a patch
of untouched ground, and trace shapes of the devil
with wild abandon.

· · · · · · · · · ▶

and when the water finally returns, it is because you
ran out of flat sand to ruin, forced to finally stop and see
the extent of your crimes before they are quietly erased.
but by then you have given up on trying to touch the ocean.
currents are deadly, and though you have been taught for years,
swimming was never in the curriculum.

· ·

I love this one for its utterable reverence in the most secular of settings.

Lauren James attends Goose Creek HS in
Goose Creek, SC. She will graduate in 2020.

Aliyah Blattner

Southridge HS, Beaverton, OR

Fruit Tree

Lover, last night my copper veined wrists wept trickles of flame
along the edges of your cobble-stoned hips. The goddess

of this Earth is confined within your candle-wick bones,
and your ankles end in torn ribbons, feet frayed.

Tell me lover, how the fruits of your youth
root themselves within your collar bones. For yesterday,

I left the house of HaShem to be greeted
by the serpentine twist of your spine. The shattered

wreckage of this graceless body glowed silver in the lamp light.
No transformation of mine has ever held such majesty.

Lover of rocking chairs and molten doves, lull me into
the serenity of your shoulder blades. When I run the pads

of my fingertips along the ridges of my own, they are mutilated
by the jagged edges. Thaw the metal lines of my body,

woman of softness. Nose your butterfly splayed palms against
my jugular, and lace my tendons with salamander slits,

submerging me into your figgy sweetness. Gentle lover,
consume me. Let faith become our kitchen, and feed me whimsy

from the whorls that mar your marrow. Lick the flecks of
rust from my hairline and trace mysticism through the keyholes

of my pores. Unlock the hidden chambers of dried petals
and overripe melancholy, that my rebirth abandoned in spite.

· · · · · · · · ·▶

162

You, lover, will forever reek of fruit trees. If I were to cut
into the meat of your abdomen, pear flesh would spill forth from

the thinly wrapped skin of your torso. Stow me away within
the crease of your elbow. And I will try to hide from the

person I am becoming. When my transcendence is actualized,
wear me from the golden chain my mother bestowed upon you

before turning to ashes in mulberry light. Someday I wish
to swing from your throat, loosely pressed against the marble

columns, so every word you speak echoes in my corrupted
heartbeat. Trace rivulets of summer wine down the slopes

of my shoulders. Let the liquid pool in your liver, metabolizing
all of me. Dripping from the corners of my eyes, honey

embeds itself into the intricacies of your ilium. And even
as I write this, the sticky amber remains tattooed to your skin.

Lover, there is no greater crime then to slay an olive tree.
Everything I touch chars obsidian, a heather film collecting

along the length of your trunk. Forgive me for the woodcutter
that I have brought into our forest of indulgence.

I thought my darkness would be enough for us both.

- -

*I've always been a sucker for figurative voyeurism; for love and lust painted with
an obscene excess of vivid imagery. The pseudo-religious undertones of this piece
give it the characteristic of the old struggle between fruitful paganism and upright,
Abrahamic purity, a struggle that still underlies most currents of modern culture.*

163

Aliyah Blattner lives in Beaverton, Oregon and attends Southridge
High School, where she will graduate in 2019. Her writing emerges
from her adamant belief in the importance of developing creative
agency and voice. Her work has been recognized by Rattle,
Scholastic, National Council of Teachers of English, and others.

Ben Sibul

Latin School of Chicago, Chicago, IL

3rd-Class

It was the third day Adek had seen her. She poked her head around the 3rd-class cabin door and peered nervously down the dimly-lit hallway that housed the ship's poorest passengers. Concealed by the shadows and filth, her bony fingers and slender arms curled carefully around the corridor entrance, and her nose seemed to twitch in rhythm with the boat's creaks and groans. The girl was used to this life; she was a nervous adventurer, always scrounging and darting and hiding. As she inched through the doorway, the candlelight danced across her face. She was pale with smudges and blemishes splashed across her cheeks, but she had kind blue eyes and golden hair that cascaded midway down her back. She reminded Adek of his own daughter, whose tenth birthday was two weeks away.

When the girl emerged fully through the doorway, Adek understood why she was being cautious. In her right hand, she held two impeccably cut slices of sourdough bread, undoubtedly stolen from a cabin or dining area in the 1st-class quarter of the Auksas. She tried unsuccessfully to conceal the bread in the folds of her tattered shirt, and when she stepped forward, Adek scanned her face for signs of guilt but saw none.

"Young lady, what are you doing there," he said. His voice was stern and commanding, as it had been for several years, but it was important for her to hear the hint of playfulness in his tone.

The girl fidgeted. Her thin fingers held the bread tightly, which was beginning to crumble and break, and her eyes darted from Adek to the grey depths of the hallway and back. Silently, she seemed to plead with him to let her run off into the darkness and disappear into the bowels of the ship.

"It's all right," he said. "You can come closer. I'm not scary. Just old." He stood slowly and pulled a chair from the wooden desk in the corner. "Come and sit a minute."

164

The girl walked toward Adek's cabin and examined him once again. Was she inspecting the wrinkles littered across his forehead? The profound creases of a life of hardship, exertion, and hunger? Was she surveying the pink scar on his cheek–the blemish he had earned in one coal mine or another? Was she looking at the fake golden chain Adriana had given to him before he left? After several minutes, the girl reached for the chair and sat.

· · · · · · · · ·▶

Adek cleared his throat. "You know that stealing is bad, yes? It goes against all the rules we've agreed to." He stared intently at the girl, trying to drive his point home as he would with his own daughter.

The girl shifted the bread to her other hand and nodded weakly.

"But sometimes, we have to break those rules in order to live." Adek smiled at the girl, and she nodded shyly. "Sometimes, we have to think of ourselves and our families before the rules."

After a few minutes of silence, Adek leaned forward again. "Where are you from?" "Warsaw," she whispered. Her voice was sad and so faint that Adek had to strain his ears to pick out and piece together again each word she muttered. He enjoyed the sound, though. Her tone was melodic and haunting, an accretion of emotion and purpose.

"It's a nice city," Adek said, running his fingers through his thin silvery hair. "And why America?"

"Mom says there's work there."

"Of course."

Adek felt impolite for asking a question he knew the answer to. The 3rd-class passengers of the Auksas were Poland's poorest; they were the forgotten, left on the streets and alleyways to fend for themselves, even during the coldest months. Adek looked at the girl's scarred hands, and he felt an unsettling pain spread throughout his body, a familiar ache that cast darkness over his thoughts. He recognized those hands. They were the hands of the malnourished children with unkempt hair and wild eyes that gathered near the butcher's shop in his neighborhood. The hands of the boys and girls who begged for change at the end of the school day. The hands of his daughters.

"Listen," Adek said. "You can run along now, but be careful." He reached behind him and pulled out a packet of dried beef from the suitcase Adriana had packed for him. "And take this, please. You'll need the protein."

The girl cupped her palms for Adek to drop the packet.

"Thank you," she said, before compelling her small, exhausted body to rise from the chair. After reaching the cabin doorway, she stopped and glanced back at Adek, flashing a weak smile, and then as if she never existed, the young girl disappeared down the foul-smelling corridor.

165

The next evening, Adek lay in bed, gazing out of the porthole on the opposite side of the room. He swept his eyes across the sea, calm and silent for the time, and he nodded farewell to the sun dipping into the water and casting an orange glow into the sky above. He wished it were this peaceful back home. He wanted Adriana and his daughters to see the seagulls perched on the deck

· · · · · · · · ▶

railings and hear the gentle rumble of the ship as it parted the waters below. Dorota and Ela, nine and eleven, would appreciate this scenery – the kind they had only seen in photographs and short films.

What time was it? Ela was probably helping her mother prepare the stew now, chopping the onions, mincing the garlic, and, if Adriana had amassed enough spare change to go to the butcher, she was washing the lamb and chicken. Dorota was most likely beginning her schoolwork, flipping through pages of mathematical equations and spelling lessons.

Leaving them was the last thing Adek wanted to do, but the thought of buying them new dolls, clothing, art supplies, pencils, and books–the things they saw through the store windows in Gdańsk but knew not to ask for–urged him to keep going. He would find a decent-paying job in America so that his wife and children could afford what they deserved: a life not governed by hunger and scarcity, but by warmth and satisfaction. Adek could already picture Dorota's radiant smile as she opened a box of new, freshly sharpened colored pencils.

As the sun disappeared beneath the waves and the orange sky morphed into a grey silhouette, Adek thought he could see the little girl's blue eyes in the distance. They were mournful and longing. Poor girl, he thought.

He pulled a withered blanket over his shoulders and closed his eyes.

In the middle of the night, Adek awoke to the shrill screams of women and children and the sudden shouts of the 1st-class gentlemen and the ship's crew. Down the hallway, lights flickered on and people emerged from their cabins, groggy and disoriented, glancing nervously at one another, fearing the worst. As the shouts grew louder and more rapid, Adek looked nervously out the window. The black waves raged against the ship's hull now, unrelenting, undeterred.

He rose from his bed, draped his nightgown over his shoulders, and followed the other passengers to the upper deck. When he arrived, he felt the gentle hum of the ship beneath his feet, he saw the black stream of coal smoke spiraling into the air, and he spotted the seagulls perched on the deck railings. At a starboard-side viewing deck, a group of passengers and sailors paced frantically along the railing, shouting at each other and motioning toward the sea.

The captain of the ship, a Lithuanian man with an unpleasant rash on his right cheek, was positioned at the front of the group, trying desperately to calm the passengers and his crew.

166

"There is nothing we can do," he said. "The water is too cold."

Adek hurried to the railing. He scanned the stretch of water visible through the ship's emergency lights, and soon discovered the urgency. One kilometer out from the ship's stern, the lifeless body rocked in the waves. In the light, he saw

Ben Sibul

strands of long golden hair glittering against the jet-black ocean backdrop. He could barely make out her bony arms and legs as she drifted away from the Auksas, rolling and turning under the cruel current.

Adek turned to the captain. "Let me go in. I know her. She was the little girl in my hallway. I can swim–"

"Absolutely not." The captain grabbed Adek by the shoulders. "The water is too cold, and you'll die as well. Don't be stupid."

Every instinct told Adek to disregard the captain, remove his nightgown and slippers, and dive head-first into the icy blackness, but deep within, he knew the captain was right. He would die along with the girl, and then who would his wife and children rely on to survive? There would be no one to feed and clothe them, to protect them from the menace of poverty and misfortune.

In an instant, he had accepted the fate of this girl–the girl who scurried through dark and dangerous places in order to survive another day. She was one of the millions of poor Poles, the 3rd-class constituents of a 3rd-class country, who spent their days toiling and running, only fortunate enough to think about the next few hours. She was among the unluckiest of the unlucky.

Adek backed slowly away from the railing, nodded to the captain, and held back tears as he pushed through the crowd of onlookers. After descending to the lower deck of the ship, he made his way through the darkness and back to his room.

When Adek closed the cabin door behind him, he fell to his knees and wept into his arm. He wept for the girl and for her misfortune, and for everyone who knew her. She was someone's daughter. But she was dead now, eliminated mercilessly from history and consciousness, and, still, the wind intensified, the waves crashed violently into the ship, and the night darkened.

Trembling, Adek climbed into his bunk. As his cries echoed in the night, the ship rumbled on.

. . . .

Ben Sibul nails these characters, these lives, in two settings and with only the most essential exposition. This is a fiction writer but there is a poet behind this story, and he's been paying very close attention to people.

Ben Sibul igraduated from the Latin School of Chicago in 2018. Born and raised in the Windy City, Ben is a die-hard White Sox fan, a deep-dish pizza addict (only if it's gluten-free), and a frequenter of Chicago's many museums and theaters. He attends Yale, and though he's unsure of what he wants to study there, he loves writing stories and poetry.

167

Temima Levy

Hasmonean HS, London, England

Breathe

The squalling primordial muck that burst through her in a torrent of pain was a child. There, see the curvature of the head, the ten perfect stubs of flesh. It's a girl-it was a girl. The pain-haze was crushing her and she gasped for something not joy and reached out her own skin that still hummed with the latent memory of pain and took back the teratoma that had hatched from her womb. Watch the mute musical of chemicals, shooting spires of hormones, the trudging line; oxytocin, dopamine, serotonin, nonapeptides thrumming up and down neural pathways. They call it love.

See the stubs elongating into fingers which could clutch a pen or clamber across the black and white ivory landscape of a piano mouth. Her mother never saw. The sparking neurons must have glitched, igniting tendons in the feet and sending the mother running from her child and the hospital and eventually, fifteen years later, under a bus.

She saw her mother the first time at the funeral. The twist in her stomach like a kicking foot might have been love. Or hunger. The cadaver wreathed in white and black bus-bruises was more beef than sapiens. The shiver was indoctrinated, not instinctive. Instinct told her to eat. The skin was maggoty-white and the bruises more purple than black, like grape-juice stains, but she still felt hungry.

Our holy father that art in heaven.

Back into the primordial muck.

The hunger was never sated. She went through different books and different beds but there was never anything to cull the ache. Rapacity simmered just under her left breast, a constant burn. The clarity of a good book or a good lay was never satisfaction, just an impermanent respite from the hunger. It was hunger that made her do it.

A bridge and a heavy rock tied tight with rope and that was it. One more soul for the reaper. But it was genetics again, because the neurons could never seem to get their job right. She left behind a son, too, wan and ill-starred. Yellow-skinned Cancer, scuttling in the shadows of a grandma's death and mother's suicide.

. . . . ➤

When he reached forty they were all taking bets, but he made it, all the way to sixty-seven and medical malpractice in a hospice smelling like mucus and cigarette smoke and apathy. His daughter, twenty-one and bound for Harvard, already level-headed equanimical came and sat his wake in Prada heels and suits she didn't clean.

That was what my mother did – she cleaned for them – steamy basins and frothing soap flakes and fingers cracking like a fault line. Too tired to scream when they blew her head off. Drunk shapes wanting cash and free thrills. It's always hunger, and they killed her but they could never be full. If this weren't what it was then I would chase down those men, cut their testicles off and stuff them down their penitent throats. Instead I got the running gene from the half-dry clothes that flapped and dripped on the sink like animal skins, and when I came to find out what was taking my mother so long to come home I ran from the meat sprawled on the ground.

Now the top of the building or the jar of opioids or the dollar razor is waiting for me. End in sight, just over the mountain of Soon. Too much living already. Too much hunger. Maybe wherever they are, all those women before me, maybe they're full now, but I don't think so.

My eulogy will be hunger.

Just breathe…

The collective eulogy of a star-crossed family, "Breathe" sews mental illness, legacy, and grief into the fabric of a society that "smells like... cigarette smoke and apathy." The racing, unpunctuated run-ons that fill the piece read like a slam poem, beating back against the urgency of time, mirroring the hunger they chronicle. We see the same story play out through a fast-forwarded generational flip book, ending finally with a narrator resigned to die in the shadow of broken lives. "maybe... all those women before me, maybe they're full now, but I don't think so. My eulogy will be hunger."

169

Temima Levy is a voracious reader who fills the time between books with writing, painting and attending Hasmonean High School, a London-based school where she is in the class of 2022. Her work has previously been published in *Teen Ink* and *Blue Marble Review*.

Maya Berardi

Avonworth HS, Pittsburgh, PA

The Word Gun Becomes

the word gun becomes
a gun itself, gathering something ugly at the back of the
throat to lurch forward, the syllable stumbling through
the mouth's dark hall like a drunk, before splitting into open air
and light, the hard 'nah,' final fatality and flick of a
tipped tongue, compact consonant tucked behind the teeth for later.

the word gun becomes
a bed sheet white like hands of the American mother who pins it
up on her backyard clothesline, waiting for the wind to
stir obedient stillness. no, not that. it hangs in wait for an
inventor, for someone sly with speakers and a projector to
show their movie over the blankness, then charge admission.

the word gun becomes
whatever it needs to be – a security alarm, a royal flush, a
    signed contract,
a main street parade, a loyal dog, a firework display, a father's voice,
    a new car,
a punctuation mark, a flexed arm, a megaphone, a crown, a trophy,
    a drug,
the tingling rush sparkling hot in veins.
the pleasure that can't be helped or named.

the word gun becomes
gloves, glaring power even though my pulse
flutters under the word's beat. a metal weight in my jaw.
a mousetrap.

The voice of the narrator here is pensive, yet powerful, as Berardi draws an intimate portrait of gun violence in America. It's eye-opening, poignant, and haunting.

Maya Berardi is from Pittsburgh, Pennsylvania. She serves as the Editor of the literary magazine 'fragments' and founder of improv poetry service 'On the Spot Poems.' Her work has also been published in *Jenny Magazine*, *The Apprentice Writer*, and *Large Print*. She will graduate from Avonworth High School in 2019.

Sandra Chen

Amador Valley HS, Pleasanton, CA

Origami Girls

Heather had only been gone a year, and yet the town feels smaller than she remembers. The world seems to turn slower, too here, and on nights like this, she can see it all dwindling to a halt. Nighttime had been different in New York, where the horns blared and the headlights blurred and the highway was a parking lot. Here, at midnight, the streets are bare. The nightlife consists of flickering fluorescent signs with two letters missing, silhouettes drowning in debt and doubt, crickets and their nighttime symphonies. Here, at midnight, the only movement is reducing. Here, at midnight, the town strangles her, constricts around her, squeezes out every last breath in clouds of white. Not that Heather minds – she's always preferred shrinking spaces.

Her house has grown out where the town has grown in. The hallways extend like swan necks; the rooms bloat with air. Now there is too much empty space in which her mother's questions drift and linger, unspoken and unanswered. In her intro biology course, Heather had learned about diffusion. Perhaps that's why she feels so hollow, the vacancy in the paper-thin rooms around her flowing into an area of lower concentration, seeping deep into her bones, trying to reach equilibrium. Or perhaps it's because she's still learning to grow into the new body prescribed to her, with all of its unwanted skin and cellulite.

Dinner tonight is a replay of days past, a cyclical gathering of familial strangers. Heather sees it all without looking. Absent nods and murmured requests. Taut mouths pulled shut with fraying string. Chopsticks in clenched fists, knuckles white as raw jasmine rice. Her little sister splits cubes of tofu into eight even pieces, her chopsticks stirring them around the cracked walls of her bowl in a skittering dance. Only one makes it into her mouth before the screech of wood against wood. She leaves the table, her footsteps amplified and heavy, her bowl thudding in the sink.

172

"You're done already, Iris?" her mother asks. "You barely ate today."

"I'm not hungry," Iris says. "Can I go?"

"Of course," she pauses. "Are you sure you're feeling okay? You haven't been eating much all week. Is there something wrong? Do you want me to – "

"Jesus Christ, Mom, I'm not a little baby. I said I wasn't hungry."

··········▶

The steely edge of Iris' voice cuts through the air and her mother's tongue. She storms out, her steps upstairs reverberating through the remnant silence, the sound waves ricocheting like bullets. Her mother shrinks before Heather's eyes, folds herself up, as if taking up less space can give her daughter more. Heather lays her hand over her mother's and feels the seismic pulsing.

"I'll talk to her."

She does not wait for the response she knows is not coming. With one last gentle squeeze of her mother's hand, one last touch of skin and ice, she leaves the table. She walks up the stairs as though she is made of paper, her steps flimsy, her chest torn, her face folded and creased so many times it is no longer readable. Iris' door is closed. Heather knocks.

"Leave me alone!"

"It's me," she says. "Can I come in?"

There is a pause on the other side. "Do I have a choice?"

Heather cracks a hesitant smile and eases open the door. Iris is curled up with her head buried into her pillow, her body sagging into the foam as if her mattress is a cloud she can fall through. Her hand still clutching the doorframe, Heather stares at Iris as if seeing her for the first time. Maybe she is. The Iris she'd left just one year ago had lived in a technicolor haze. Where Heather was pale, Iris had always been blue-tinted fingers and ruby-stained lips. But this Iris is fading, her body translucent against the too-white walls, white like plastic knives, white like bleached teeth, white like a hospital. Heather wants to stitch up the wilted petals in front of her, but all she has is quivering hands and too much blood.

Iris sits up. "What do you want?"

Her words are empty, tired as the rest of her. Heather's feet respond before her mouth can, inching her toward the bed. Her hand reaches to wrap her sister's, but Iris recoils, her fingers withdrawn into a fist. Heather lets her head and stomach drop with her arm.

"Why didn't you finish your dinner?" Heather asks, her voice like a wisp of wind.

"How many times do I have to say I'm not hungry?"

"Come on, Iris. You don't have to lie to me."

Iris laughs, venom dripping from her lips. "Like you never lied to me?"

"I – this isn't about me."

"Isn't it?"

· · · · · · · ·▷

Heather trains her eyes on the floor to ground herself, and they catch the light reflecting from a glass corner extending out from underneath the bed. Everything stops.

"What is that."

Her words are not meant as a question; she knows exactly what the glass pane is, can still feel it under her bare feet and leaden bones, can still see the digital numbers climbing, each black dash flashing. When Iris silently bends over to push the sharp edge back, Heather feels as though its glass shards have punctured her. She had seen all of the dinner dancing, all of the footwork around food, but she had not wanted to believe her little sister had learned her routine. Now neither of them moves or talks or breathes. But Heather sees and she knows and she almost laughs, because it's funny, how they both ended up this way. Two crumpled origami girls with crumbling glass hearts.

. . . .

Yes. The quiet yet vivid tone seems to reflect the way eating disorders are treated in our society; at the same time, it contrasts with the ugliness and severity of this illness.

Sandra Chen

the dancer

you are eight years old, standing in a dim-lit bathroom.
turning to the side, your eyes rest on the curve of your
stomach. your belly stretches against the thin spandex
of a black leotard, the protruding arc disrupting the line
of your body. you press the palm of your hands against it,
apply pressure, open your lungs and hold your breath for
as long as you can. when the air leaves, you do, too,
turning off the lights before closing the door.

you are twelve years old, rigid in the corner of a studio.
today, the teacher takes proportions to send to costume
tailors. the yellow metal strip wraps around your chest first,
then waist, then hips. you suck in as much as you can,
pretend your stomach is a vacuum. the lack of oxygen blurs
the syllables of the numbers you don't want to hear. as the
metal presses against your inner thigh, its cold imprint reminds
you that the length of your legs is too short, the width too long.
when the teacher brings the tape measure from your left shoulder,
down between your thighs, and back up, wrapping around the
span of your torso like caution tape, you start to think
your body is the scene of a crime you can't escape.

you are sixteen years old, practicing grand pliés at the bar.
in preparation, you exhale with your arms and open your feet
to first position, legs squeezed together. the girls around you
do the same, only it isn't the same, because they are cut like
sticks, long and lean. when you bow down and wedge your
thigh in your hands to force turnout, lumps rise between your
fingers. when you rise, your eyes trail off your fingertips to the
omnipresent mirror. now, you no longer look toward your core,
having long ago learned how to press your ribs into your skin
and create a concave curve. if only suffocating could slim your
legs. your gaze turns methodical, as if performing surgery
on the girl in the mirror. you mark parts of her for excision,

· · · · · · · · ·▶

prescribe contortions as medication. lifted neck, softened arm,
straightened knee, tucked tailbone, elongated spine. still, it's
all wrong. everything is misaligned, jutting out or
caving in, blotches swollen with cellulite. every part of her.

Yes. For another girl who started agonizing over her protruding belly at
eight years old, Chen's words ring true and deep. I'm not a dancer,
but the toxically cultured art form serves as brilliant frame for this exposé
on a society that convinces so many girls and women that they're "all wrong."

Sandra Chen is in the class of 2019 at Amador Valley High
School in Pleasanton, California. Her work has been
recognized by the Scholastic Art and Writing Awards and the
National Poetry Quarterly, and can be found in the *Vassar Review*,
Ellipsis Zine, and the *Rising Phoenix Review*, among others.

Isabelle Edgar

Falmouth HS, Falmouth, MA

Let's Go

One step at a time. We sat on the stoop with the ivy growing around our toes. Brown green grass, and shade, always shade. Grandma picked a pile of dandelions and piled them beside our knees, yellow dust beneath my fingernails.

One step at a time. In the yard he raked the red orange leaves into piles. Piles higher than my head. I listened to the sound of the deadness becoming one.

One step at a time, I weaved my rainboots in and out of blue gray puddles, watching the way crystals disappear as they struck surface. Red hood sheltered my eyelashes from the rain.

"Life loves to be taken by the lapel and told, "I'm with you kid, let's go."

Let's go. Take my hand and we'll go to the cusp of the atmosphere, the edge of the ocean.

Grandma wove the stems of each flower into the next. The yellow fluff forming a chain, my little hands watching, mirroring. She laced one behind my ear, tangled in my hair.

Dad knelt beside me and pointed at the colors. Painting the auburn glow into my brain. Nature's confetti.

I hovered over the surface of the water. Watching a pair of brown eyes too big for a small face beneath a red hood appear below me. The surface quivered and I smiled at the looking glass.

Let's go. Take my hand and we will swim to the sand at the bottom of the sea, the tip of the peninsula.

It created a circle of sunshine. She lifted it like a web and placed it within the strands of my hair. I looked up at the blueness in her eyes and she said "just like the fairies."

177

It was a pool, a cushion, just waiting. I ran as fast and jumped as high as small legs allow into a sea of leaves. Dad dusted them from my laughing eyes and said "nature's confetti."

It appeared to be an ocean of sorts. I stomped waves into the sea, swallowed by the redness of the raincoat. The puddle danced away reflections as I hummed "i'm singin' in the rain."

Let's go. Take my hand and we will grow into our shoes, learn to see through cracked sunshine.

I didn't want to grow up. To drift away from fairies, confetti and puddles. To understand fully. I wanted to understand partially. But life likes to take you by the lapel and tell you that it's time to move on.

I wanted to be submerged in magic; soaked, saturated, simply believing the things that so many people say are not worth believing in.

He took my hand and the old telescope that has been in the basement for years and we walked in the nightness. We sat with our backs against the white canoe. He told me to look into the lens at the blankness. Nothing was clear.

"... Science popularizers have said humans are made of stardust, and now, a new survey of 150,000 stars shows just how true the old cliché is"

Inside the creases of your palms, on the tips of your eyelashes, in your veins, stars lie sleeping. We are a melting pot of atoms.

"Life loves to be taken by the lapel and told, "I'm with you kid, let's go.""

There's a certain magic to letting go. To letting the earth swallow you up and hold you in the palm of its hand, to be open. Open to believing because there are so many things that we just don't know and so many things that we do know that are magical.

In a sense I believe. I still make dandelion crowns and watch reflections sway in puddles, I still look through the telescope and think how the blurred images are part of me. How we don't know what's up there in the mountainous array of space. I still want to take love by the lapel and do as it asks.

. . . .

I'm willing to fight for this piece. It's stunning, beautiful, and moving.

178

Isabelle Edgar is a senior at Falmouth High School in Falmouth, MA (class of 2019). She loves poetry, contemporary ballet, hiking in beautiful places and the ocean.

Haemaru Chung

Trinity School, New York, NY

Reverie

After it slips,
I can see the scene.
Clean cracks,
windchimes on a winter
morning.
Chalky slivers,
a startled flock of geese.
Riptides around
ceramic reefs.

But I flinch
as the cup shatters.
Look down
to see a broken gift
and bitter tea
that soaks into my socks.

Wonderfully tender and sweet, balancing beautiful language and brevity in the best way possible. The simple descriptions transport the reader to a morning, perhaps in March – crisp, fresh, almost holding your breath for something about to happen – spring, perhaps. Or the shattering of a cup.

179

Yacht

I slide over silver,
enter the eye of the color wheel.
Silent laborers plow sands
under weighted shells,
white, ephemeral ribbons.
I rest against coarse walls,
observe the silent chaos
as colors blink away.

A boat rumbles above.
Its underbelly interrupts
the light's rhythm,
energizes debris,
an ugly constellation.

Plastic wrings the fish,
a deadly headdress.
Shells peel and rip,
exposing tender skin.
Oil seeps in lungs and veins,
thickens vibrant eyes
to foggy glass.
Red coral bleaches pink,
then white, then ash.

I love the imagery – especially in the last stanza where it's appropriately disturbing. I also appreciate how concise the poem is while still getting quickly and efficiently to its point.

Haemaru Chung is a senior at Trinity School in New York City and an alumnus of the Iowa Young Writers Studio. He received the National Scholastic Art and Writing Awards, Hippocrates Young Poets Prize, Gannon University Writing Awards, among others. His works have been published in numerous literary magazines, including _Rising Phoenix Review_, _L'Ephemere Review_, _Ricochet Review_, _Louisville Review_, and _Snapdragon_.

Maytreecia Harriell

Booker T. Washington Magnet HS, Montgomery, AL

Turbulence

Consider us on an airplane.
Drifting through cloud nine,

We're in our Honeymoon Phase
Where I can't stop smiling every time I see you,
And you me.
Where every thought I have is
you are the moon,
and I your stars
and we're in this cloud.

But then
comes the turbulence.
And you, my captain,
Come online to tell me fasten my seatbelt and enjoy the show.
Enjoy the show?
This is an argument in itself.
How dare you tell me what to do!
You are NOT my father.
And how can I enjoy the show when I'm deathly afraid and
        you're nowhere to be found.
Your retort is a maddening expression of confusion.
But then you bring me food and I luuuuv you again.
This is the cycle of us.
You make me mad and you bring me food and you
        make me happy again.
This is our HONEYMOON PHASE.

181

Well not exactly...

I-I-I

I kind of lied.

A-A-A

And I want to tell you the truth.

N-N-N

Now.

You know how I said we were on a plane?

Well – we were actually in a classroom.

And you know how I said we were on cloud nine?

Well – we were on the ground,

And you were thirteen feet away from me.

On TV, again.

Maytreecia Harriell, back again with a little drop of weirdly profound humor to remind us to lighten the heck up. Like her piece in our last volume, I think this poem provides a break from the typical labored, meaningful, obscure poetry we're used to and brings issues of contemporary American youth to light through humor. We could always use a little more of Maytreecia.

Maytreecia Harriell graduated from Booker T. Washington Magnet High School in Montgomery, Alabama where she was in the Creative Writing Magnet. Aside from writing, Maytreecia enjoys photography and cinematography. She is currently a Creative Media Major at the University of Alabama. When she grows up she wants to be a screenwriter.

Kouro-Maïram Baro

Lycée les Pierres Vives, Le Bon-Sauveur HS, Yvelines, France

Conversation Among Wolves

Run little wolf,
From those hands that forced
Their way into
You.

Escape little fighter,
The crushing ferocity of the world
Which leaves you
Troubled.

Flee little being,
The demons of your mind and how they taunt you,
Urging you to die.

Turn away little human,
From those aching memories,
Those regrets and what ifs.

Little, little, little…
When did I become so dismissive?
There should be no romance in surviving pain.

In truth,
You are not little, nor are you a coward.

In order to save your life,
Just this one time,
You must put yourself first.
This time, choose to rescue You.

I trust that you try to break free
From that which pushes to govern you.

I encourage you to keep going, and to search
For the keys of your kingdom,
Even if nothing else remains,
Where you once conquered,
All the fears and shame.

Are you aware of your beating heart?
If so,
Maybe you actually are not what is broken.

Could what you feel
Be the sensation of your floating organs
Swimming in the vastness of you?

Grasp onto these words,
If you're willing to accept
An alternative, where everything that is wrong,
Isn't your fault.

Isn't that a hard-earned revelation?

I understand how it feels
To be caught in someone's paws,
Cut by thorns, over and over.

That is precisely why I am here to reassure you.

There is no miracle solution to
Setting yourself free
But to grab everything you have and are,
And to keep walking through it all.

Remember, you are but human, you are still breathing.

More days in the unknown await.
Though I agree that the bad days aren't over yet,
Will you just try to forgive your shortcomings?

Once you've made it through the halls of life
As narrow as they get,

· · · · · · · · · ➤

Through the angst and despair,
The surprises and successes
I pray you close your eyes
And smell all that is alive around you.

You are no little being,
Oh, silent fighter,
Drained soul,
Courageous survivor.

Along the lines,
Did you think of how
You endure and are here, still,
Despite all that has tried to end you.
You see, your resilience screams alive better than anything
            else could.

. . . .

Somehow urgent and reassuring at the same time, this poem focuses on the hardship of survival, but also reminds readers of the quiet strength that it takes to survive. "Conversation Among Wolves" reminds readers that even if they've been through a lot, they are still breathing, and that counts for something.

Kouro-Maïram Baro will graduate from Le Bon-Sauveur high school in 2019. She was born in France and then lived in the United-States, Saudi Arabia and Senegal. She currently resides in France, and perhaps needless to say is planning on traveling more. Outside of literature and spoken word poetry, she swims and jogs and cares for her pet hamster.

Emily Dehr

Atherton HS, Louisville, KY

The Spaces Between, a runner up for the 2017 Claudia Ann Seaman Award for Creative Nonfiction, is printed here because an error on our part kept it from publication in Polyphony HS 2017 (vol. XIII). It was accepted for publication during Emily's senior year at Atherton High School.

The Spaces Between

It is dark outside. Stars are only visible in small cities, but here we have a never-ending supply of mosquitos and cicadas that never cease to sing their songs, or cry deep from their throats. I haven't figured out which one it is yet. I sit locked in my car in the driveway of my house and stare at the window that refuses to roll down. I stay there for ten minutes, twenty, sometimes an hour, sometimes more. Yes, I have things to do. Yes, I should go inside, but I close my eyes instead. I am there however long it takes to inhale enough air to make it through the night, to remember to unbuckle my seatbelt, to have the strength to actually do it. I have never rushed inside the house. There is something about the transition period, the moments that don't count in the big picture, the seconds in between, that are my escape.

Humans spend an average one-third of their free time watching TV, and 67% of that is reality television. Engrossing ourselves in someone else's life, whether it be that of a dumbed-down over-paid model or a drug addict needing therapy from a "doctor", intrigues society. We dive into the scenery around us and become that world, and bigger TV screens are desired for easier exploration of delusions. Fulfillment is the goal, but contentment is dangerous. America wants to be happy, but we will never be free - from ourselves.

I admit that I occasionally watch television, but I prefer a different kind of escape. I sometimes sit on my bed doing nothing but staring at the wall. It is a yellow a little too bright for my taste, but my sister liked the color. I study it. I need to get up to brush my teeth and change my clothes and it gets late, but I am obsessed with stretching out the transition period. The moments that don't exist after they end. The moments that will not be remembered. Just like when the minute hand ticks and the show is finally over, I will eventually be pushed back into this chaotic world. My TV always took a few extra seconds to turn on, and that is when I find my mind wandering with a chain no longer attached.

·········▶

I find memories in TV shows that I didn't know existed. Favorite birthday parties will always be remembered and our best friend's name is engrained in our brains, but the experiences we have that result in no outstanding and everlasting significance are where the truth resides. Humans are obsessed with "finding themselves" and entering the "real world", but forcing our internal clocks to stop and intertwine their hands, entangling themselves together in an arranged love, expose what we didn't know was behind a foggy stained glass. I sit in my car an extra few minutes when I notice a lack of stars and remember the telescope, now dusty, I used to look through as a child.

I sit in my car, I turn on my TV, and I stare at my wall to deviate from the path of self. There are moments in between when life slows down. The second of comprehension right after the light turns green, the exhale following the lift of the bars when the train has passed and counting cars has become old. There is something in the nothingness that holds a precious piece of life unattainable anywhere else. There is something in the nothingness that unlocks a memory so precious that it can only stand to be forgotten.

I believe my first memory to be when I was three years old. It felt like a Tuesday, and it was just past my bedtime. My kid-sized white frame bed was right in the middle of the bedroom, next to my sister's bed that was too big for me to even climb on. The carpet was too light and the walls were never painted. I moved my Tweety Bird cased pillow to the opposite side of the bed that night. There was a dark purple T-shirt with big white letters I used to wear all the time. It hung up in my closet on a thin white plastic hanger. The world was giant back then.

I kept the shirt with me that night, gripping it tight in clenched fists and ignoring my sister's curious glares. It was the first time I ever buried my face into a shirt and inhaled deeply, as if the worn-out cotton fibers were a better substitute for oxygen. It smelled like comfort, like protection, like my mom. I heard footsteps and stuffed it under my pillow. My dad walked in to kiss us goodnight, and he somehow knew it was there. He yanked it away and hung it up high where I could never reach. "Goodnight." I missed my mother's smell and cried myself to sleep. I was little and didn't think to remember, I would see her in the morning.

I flip the channel. I don't think that memory is very accurate and I am not sure it happened at all to begin with. I do, however, remain sleeping with my pillow on that side of the bed. I flip the channel. One time my sister and I drank straight lemon juice to see who could last the longest. I won. I flip the channel. I land on the memory of the time I skinned my knee skating in front of my grandparents. Cracks in the sidewalk are dangerous. I flip the channel to the memory of Honey Buns in the morning and a hindsight bias of new tennis-shoes on a shiny elementary school tiled floor. No wonder sitting in front of the TV is so tempting.

187

Emily Dehr

However, many nights I remain in my car instead. I think of empty spaces in books before the next chapter, the millisecond our eyes close to blink, the moment of silence before a new song plays on an old favorite CD, the second the screen turns black, silence in between heartbeats, the space in between each chicken-scratched letter, pauses between both harsh and soft words, the sound right before a slamming door, the second before the plane takes off, the moment before a comet is united with the earth, the inexplicable space in between parts of an atom, the flipping of TV channel memories. These are the moments where souls reside. This is where we find escape.

I lock the door and my head finds the steering wheel, my hands on the dashboard, feet under the pedals, I never move them myself. But every now and then, usually at night, I turn on the ignition and I drive. I do not stop at stop signs, speeding all the way to the highway, where there are no pauses and streetlights illuminate the lines on the road. Finally, I am free.

This piece is like a sigh, composed of the empty space that fills the gaps in our lives yet remains unnamed and unnoticed, as if it never existed. The author demonstrates a mature and polished control of prose and a strong understanding of the effects of language and structure.

188

Emily Dehr graduated from Atherton High School in 2017 and is currently studying English at Northern Kentucky University. She loves both reading and writing and has been doing both since she was young.

Meenakshi Jani

Worthington Kilbourne HS, Columbus, OH

Spaces

heyyyyyy, my boy here wants to
fuck you.
he laughs.
you are a delectable assembly
of bones and breasts
to him.

he can see the spaces
between the rungs of your ribcage you
counted
in the mirror this morning.
he slithers between them and gets
next to your heart,
no matter that it
jumps
and inches away, pounding
so as not to feed him your blood.

that laugh
is the way he makes space,
takes space,
the way he unzips your
insides with his eyes.
his gaze punctures your lungs
which balloon before
collapsing and you're gasping while he
laughs
at the bone-breast-head he thinks you are,
and you're wiping the anger off the edges

189

· · · · · · · · · ➤

of your cracked lips to keep it from spilling
over, for boiling blood makes him more spaces.

you can read between the laugh lines:
cracks that, if pulled apart, would break open space.
but if he knows you can read, he knows you can see.
so you train your gaze on the floor, collect the bashed
books and broken rib bones,
shield the scraps of yourself that remain
with your aching,

pounding brain
and count your steps force your face
to vacate soothe your stinging sores
search for a space you can keep
safe

....

*There's a rawness and vulnerability here that took me completely
by surprise. It goes from vulgar to poetic in the blink of an eye,
and it never tries to be anything but the ugliness it tells of.*

Meenakshi Jani will graduate in 2019 from Worthington Kilbourne
High School in Columbus, Ohio. Her work has appeared in the
journal *Flip the Page*, she has attended the Kenyon Review
Young Writers' Workshop, and she edits for *Polyphony Lit*. She
dances, plays piano and violin, and engages in political activism.

Aniela Cohig

Nyack, NY

ode to a cup of earl grey tea

at six-thirty-seven am you
wait listlessly for me
on the sticky kitchen table
steam performing a wispy
silver ballet in the frigid
morning air.

Mixed with oozing orange
honey, tepid milk swirls,
engulfs the soupy brown
in thick layers of white
and the palest grey
coating
my tongue with a bitter sip.

You masquerade as a friend sometimes,
scalding and sprinkled with
sugar and warm green leaves that
stick to steaming innards of a
cracked peach colored mug

but you're a monster

All your own, hissing as you
slither down my endless throat
with a sickly sweet hatred
that sizzles within me.

You feign well-meaning,

191

I know, laced with caffeine to
pry open my filmy yellow
eyes and rouse me out of a dream
I cannot seem
to remember

but I recoil at your touch,

my skin prickling and quivering,
my frantic heart
thudding in the fleshy
prison of my chest.

And you have propped

up my pitiful body for so long,
made me a husk without
your ever present swish
and so

i don't say no.

....

*There's something really powerful at work not so deeply buried. I once had a teacher
tell me that if something seemingly arbitrary is described with intense detail and you
don't know why, you're missing something. I think that's at case here. I'm not sure
exactly what the author is getting at here, but there clearly is artistic license at work.*

192

Aniela Cohig is a student at Hastings High School in Hastings-
on-Hudson, New York, which she will graduate from in 2020.
When she's not writing poetry, she enjoys writing prose,
drinking excessive amounts of tea, and petting her cat.

Rukmini Kalamangalam

Carnegie Vanguard HS, Houston, TX

culture adapts to survive in hostile environment by killing itself

i. culture, trapped

Rainwater collects in a birdbath & he chiseled this home too. Mosquito
mispronouncing her own name. Daughter wriggling through screened
window. Mite, son guilty enough to stay. Chains a tongue too thick to move.
Consecration as blood tie. Feast as dusty tablecloth & intermittent arm tremor.
Blood & body as neglected ember. Hand-knotted rug as fluttering kindling.
Stained glass as catalyst. Flame as rainbow & decay in fast forward. & before,
the house: still & forgetting how to hold. His sleep filled. Sand in his mouth
and bricked ceiling. & now, the corpse. Wick blackening stretcher sheets.
The house's facade sags like a rotten onion. Layers falling off into the lawn.
Demolition thumbing into soft bloat. Vulturous cranes swoop in to consume.
If they find his body it'll be buried underneath the house with a trapdoor
through which children swarm. Even they come in for the night. A dying kitchen
releasing stuffed air. Entropic heat. A fireplace. A dead maestro still conducting

ii. culture as trappings

no energy. Electricity crackling in a rubber coffin. Bring back the chorus. Pull
out the strobe lights and sunglasses. Let the slaves harvesting rubber come
back from the dead. Let their limbs refuse to resurrect. Let each of them pick
an electron to dance on. Cirque du Soleil but more grotesque. More pirates
from the Caribbean. Oh, isn't this fun? They can breathe through finger width
spaces between ribs. They'd kill synchronized swimming. Can you imagine?
Put aerosol under leagues of water pressure and watch them explode like coke
cans. Let there be no proton. Let them not coalesce. Let us save the protomartyrs
building cryo chambers out of balsa wood and enslave new peoples

193

. . . . ➤

iii. a trap, culture

as urn pouring ash into river. Ancestral remains polluted shadows long and wide as medieval spires. Cries as church bells. Deconstructed crosses feeding pyres. In the Philippines they nail a new Jesus to the cross every year except it's been the same man volunteering for 28 Fridays and no one calls him good. Buddha dies from starvation each time we forget he is still begging. He waves to our herd and half the disciples are instantly transported to Nirvana. (Who could choose to believe in death?) The other half are reborn as poets, editing the same piece as Sisyphus rolling the printing block up the mountain, trailing grey beards in teeming rainwater.

. . . .

If you're looking for a neat narrative through line, here, you won't find it. This is not a literal poem. It paints in feelings, in disconcerting shadows and misfired neurons that connect physics and history and pop culture into a restless dream that echoes the subject's deathly sleep. Beautiful and scattered and complete.

Rukmini Kalamangalam graduated from Carnegie Vanguard High School (Houston, TX) in 2018 and is currently a freshman at Emory University. She was named 2018 Youth Poet Laureate of the Southwest. She has been published by the *Houston Chronicle*, *ABC 13 Visions*, *Houston Public Media*, *Mutabilis Press*, and *The Apprentice Writer*.

Malaika John

Bentonville HS, Bentonville, AK

A White Girl with Particularly Dark Skin

What makes me black?

I thought it was the way the sun bounced off my cocoa skin,
The perpetually tangled knots of my nappy hair,
My darker than night brown eyes,
My West African Heritage

But apparently
It's not

It means being tough,
gangsta.
and occasionally
letting the forbidden word slip.

Instead of studying for school
I'm supposed to listen to rap
on my way to buy pot from
Trayvon,
The Crips member next door

I can stop to wave at
Shaniqua
and her four kids
who have four different fathers,

hoping that the policeman
watching me, protecting me,
won't smell the weed in my pocket,
the criminal nature in my blood

195

as I walk the streets
of my crime-infested, ghetto-ass neighborhood

And maybe someday my dad will come back

And I can tell them that isn't me
That I'm just
a suburban chick
who likes to read
and to write

But the only response they can formulate
The only plausible explanation
The only logical conclusion
For me,
the exception –

Is that
you must be white.

··

*This one pulls no punches. It goes after and exposes the harmful
expectations America puts on people of color, the rigidity of our society
that allows race to limit the possibilities of identity and marginalizes every
black voice, as often for fitting the stereotypes than for not.*

Malaika John will graduate from Bentonville HS in Bentonville, Arkansas in 2020. Before Bentonville, she had the great experience of living in another country for two years. She is part of her school's debate team which she thinks will serve her well as she plans to become a lawyer.

Paul Michaud

Groton School, Nashville, TN

 2018 Claudia Ann Seaman Award Runner Up for Fiction

Advanced Fiction

The consensus among the members of the University English Department was that, while Melanie's writing sample was neither diverse nor inclusive, it sure was a good study of some sensitive white kids who went to college and found themselves sadder than they thought possible. This sadness was partly because the characters in her story had had a (predictably) sheltered upbringing in a (predictably) upper-middle-class town in Connecticut. The English department also agreed that, while Melanie's story didn't tackle any issues currently plaguing the country (racism, division, gun violence, fracking, etc), it revealed things at just the right moment. Things like that the main character Ida's boyfriend of three years was cheating on her with another girl from their shared hometown when they (Melanie and the boyfriend) went back home from Wesleyan for break. Or that Melanie had never noticed that the other girl was in a picture on her dorm room wall. Or that it was a class photo, featuring her boyfriend Chad and this other girl, standing next to each other at graduation. The general consensus was also that Melanie's word choice was understated and powerful, and her use of commas was, to quote one professor, "exemplary." And so Melanie was admitted to ENG400: Advanced Fiction.

She got the email on a Friday night. She was at a party getting what her boyfriend Brody called "daunted." Sometimes Melanie felt like Brody was a fraud but at some moments she could feel his straining sincerity. She could virtually hear his brain whirring at 200 rpm, trying to impress her. *Did you read* The Sun Also Rises? *Daunted is from* The Sun Also Rises! Melanie was almost on her third drink but nowhere near daunted. Some bass-boosted music was playing from a speaker in the corner. There was a big, rusty boat in the middle of the room filled with beer cans. Someone from the frat they were at had spray painted it with the title of a Jimmy Buffet song: boat drinks. Melanie could see Brody out of the corner of her eye. He was jumping around in a cutoff tee shirt, waving his arms like something she didn't have a word for yet. She checked

197

⋯⋯⋯➤

her phone and saw that she had gotten into the class. Her hands were shaking a little as she checked the other recipients of the email. It was a lot of people she didn't know.

She started her first story that night in her room, still a little drunk. It was about a high schooler who read too much. She titled it *Bookish*. All the main character did was wander around his prep-school campus and cherry-pick lines from books to describe people. The main character, Alton, had a math teacher who was "one of those men who reach such an acute limited excellence at twenty-one that everything afterward savors of anti-climax." The headmaster was "Hemingwayesque." He called his physics teacher Yorick. It was a bad story, and it lacked plot development, but Melanie had worked hard on it. So she was surprised when, after reading B*ookish* aloud in workshop, she looked up to find nine faces simpering back at her, full of pity. The professor asked the class what they thought worked in the story, to start. Seven hands shot up, and Melanie felt like crying.

Class progressed. Her classmates were all wearing Birkenstocks and held gel pens in their right hands. A few hadn't showered. She thought about how Brody sometimes strained, and how the main character of *Bookish* sometimes strained, too, but how both Brody's and Alton's straining combined was nothing next to everyone in class. Everyone was interrupting each other and rephrasing what had already been said. Someone described Alton as "ruminative." Someone else described the prep school as "sumptuous." A third person said that the story didn't seem real. Some others snapped in agreement, and Melanie became aware of just how many people had read something she had made up.

That night, Melanie called her mother and told her that she wanted to come home. Her mother asked what was wrong.

"I don't know," Melanie said.

"You've never wanted to come home before," said her mother.

"I know," Melanie said.

"Well, what's wrong, then?"

"I don't want to see Brody anymore."

"Oh."

Of course, this wasn't true. Brody annoyed Melanie sometimes but never enough that she didn't want to see him. Whenever they drove to college together, he would invent little songs for all the towns they passed. She knew his bedroom as well as she knew hers. But coming home still seemed the right thing to do, and so, with apologies to her teachers she did.

At home, she took the opportunity to write the second of three stories for the class. It was longer, since she had more time. Sort of vindictively, Melanie thought, it was hyper-real. The counter in the main character's off-campus apartment was dusty and scattered with poppy seeds. The character (named Melanie, too) wore grey-green pants, like Melanie herself. She went to Wesleyan. She had the beginnings of a drinking problem, as did her boyfriend (referred to in the story only as B – – .) Story-Melanie went to her political science classes and wrote papers and went to the dining hall and ate alone. The story took place in the winter and Story-Melanie was sad. Not really so much sad as in constant, screaming pain about the problems of the world. Story-Melanie thought about all the issues that the first story – the one she'd used to get into the class – hadn't dealt with. She thought about how screwed-up the system of American higher education was. She thought about how no one was really genuine. She called her best friend back at home twice a day. She refused therapy because therapists were frauds.

This time, in class, no hands went up, and everyone looked at their shoes when the professor asked for the good parts of the story. The professor stopped Melanie after class and asked if she needed help. Melanie said that Story-Melanie was a character. The professor said that, in that case, Melanie should think about why she named Story-Melanie what Melanie had named her.

The third story was two pages, single-spaced. It followed the plot of Macbeth, but it was set in Seattle. Macbeth was a short-haired female barista who saw a copy of Atlas Shrugged hovering in front of her face instead of a knife. Lady Macbeth was her long-haired boyfriend whose blood-stained hands were actually stained with tomato juice from canning tomatoes for Saturday morning's farmer's market. Everyone laughed in class, including her professor. Melanie joined in, but she hadn't meant for it to be funny.

When she got back from class, Brody was asleep in her bed smelling like cologne. Melanie changed out of her hot sweater, slipped out of her dorm room in flip-flops, and went to the campus Career Center, on the third floor of a huge concrete building.

She hadn't ever been there before. There was molded, bright-colored plastic furniture everywhere. The motivational posters on the walls were cheesy and sincere but didn't really strain. The receptionist was walking on a treadmill desk, wearing yoga pants and running shoes.

"Hi!" Said the receptionist.

Melanie became suddenly aware of how she looked in the office. She was wearing her flip-flops, a dirty pair of jean shorts, and a flannel shirt tied at the bottom. She was carrying a canvas backpack. In her back pocket was a copy of a Graham Greene book. She fled without explanation, out the door and across the street and back up into her room.

When she opened her door, Brody was still asleep in the bed. Melanie sat down on the couch and thought about things. About how "Brody" didn't sound so much different than "Chad." About how her mother had talked to her after she had walked past Brody and that other girl on the street. About how Brody had basically cried while telling her how he had only kissed the other girl, and only once. About how clever it was to add the detail about the class picture into her story, even though it hadn't really happened. She hadn't been proud of the original story like she'd been proud of the ones she'd reached deep inside and made up. It had seemed more natural, though; she hadn't been able to find any flow since.

But now there was nothing for her to say. Pages of gently worded comments piled on her desk. Melanie could skim a few from where she was sitting on her couch. She thought about how you had to word your comments. *"I liked this, but…" "Nice descriptions, but…" "Good job! I'd like to see…"* Melanie was glad no one had read the first story – the one she had used to get into the class – but she also knew it had been the best one, because it was all true. She had changed the names, of course, and fucked around a little with the timeline, but there it was, all of it. And she was glad that no one had put comments in the margins of that one.

<hr>

I fell in love with it and immediately saved it to my desktop. I love the start, I love the pace, I love the joke about comma use, I love the idea of a litmag publishing a piece about an author working through feedback. Oooooooh. There's something here that I think most of our authors and readers will fall in love with – it's eerily relatable.

200

Paul Michaud lives in Nashville, Tennessee. He attended the Groton School in Groton, MA, from which he graduated in 2018.

Cia Gladden

St. Ignatius HS, Chicago, IL

violent ends

the dogs of war defiled this world
with a bloodlust of which unfurled
upon the whims of flaxen crowns
once they grew bored of wine and gowns

something wicked emerged within
their dreadful cove of blood and sin
for even as the shackles fell
newborn lords sang, "it is a knell!"

time's subjects watched sweet princes grow,
maturing not to swan but crow
so throne reared venom; poison bloom'd
while mortals paid no heed to doom.

affliction, 'namoured of our kings,
preyed on each soul and clipped their wings;
these flightless humans stumbled forth,
unable to find jeweled worth.

a pound of flesh each paid in turn;
the angels writhed as their grace burn'd,
for humans had giv'n up their pride
to have the wealth they so desired.

a mad idolatry was crowned
yet no gold rested on her brow;
instead, she dressed in fiscal zeal;
the bloodless collar was her seal.

they craved no other; she was 'nough
to quake the church, replace the calf,

. . . . ➤

play 'O Mistress Mine' (each chord),
and be worshipp'd, kiss'd, lov'd, ador'd.

sick in fortune, their Earth did wail,
but obtuse men cried, "Hail! Hail! Hail!"
to worship Wealth, their dirty god;
meanwhile, their souls fell to her jaws.

is that not strange? riches swallow
from mortal to bright Apollo,
so, muse of fire, I beg of you
to sheath your blade and start anew.

the violence of her gory power
has slashed to shreds the Earth's last hour;
they feign allure of Helen of Troy,
but silv'r and gold themselves destroy.

Lines found in *Romeo and Juliet, Julius Caesar, Macbeth, Henry IV, Hamlet, The Merchant of Venice, Measure for Measure, Cymbeline, Twelfth Night, The Two Gentlemen of Verona, Love's Labour's Lost, Much Ado About Nothing, Henry V, A Midsummer Night's Dream.*

. . . .

Absolutely phenomenal. This poem was beautifully crafted and weaved superbly.

202

Cia Gladden is a member of the class of 2019
at St. Ignatius College Prep in Chicago, IL.

Claire Quan

Deerfield, MA

Bone

I plead of thee: refuse the course of mind,
For fickle is mem'ry in matters gray.
Though strands of code through which we wind do bind,
Against the creed of time they have no say.
O! Ever I bemoan the tides betwixt, Churned
by Mnemosyne with potions lethe. How to
thy look can eye and heart affix,
If fronds shall bud and wilt as thy doth breathe?
Shadowed I see thy wings unfurl — first flight;
 Each miss'd soar my heart from far abrade,
I mark thy milestones miles away, with fright
That from thy parted lips my name doth fade.

And though cruel fate, divide, has since been sewn,
Unstitch us same, brother, 'til barren bone.

It's simply a beautiful and brave poem about love, memory, and separation.

Claire Quan was born in Singapore and raised in Shanghai. She
is currently in her junior year at Deerfield Academy (class of 2020)
where she serves as an editor on the school newspaper and literary
magazine. Her work has also been published in *Shanghai Daily*,
the *Interlochen Review*, and the *Little Brown House Review*.

Polyphony Lit Editorial Pipeline

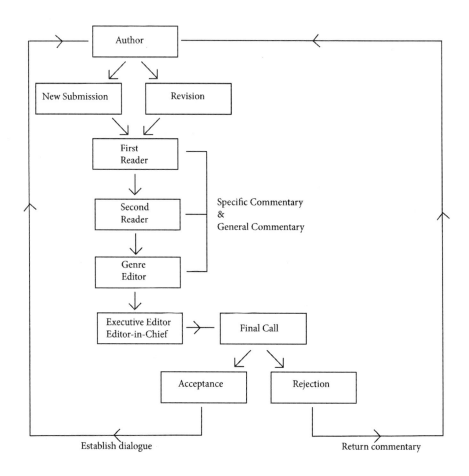

All submissions (if sent in by the early deadline), whether accepted or rejected, go through this editorial cycle. The Managing Editor merely forwards the pieces. Second readers, genre editors, executive editors and the editor-in-chief are responsible not only for editing and commenting on the submission, but for editing the commentary of the readers and editors before them as well. Most acceptances go through an in-house editorial process. In these cases the Editor-in-Chief or an executive editor works with the poet/author before coming to an agreement on the final version of the submission.